First self-publish(

Copyright (

The right of Lucy Light to be identified as the Author of the Work has been asserted by her in accordance with the Copyright, Design and Patents Act 1988.

Paperback ISBN 9798643714309

All rights reserved

This book might not be your cup of tea but trust me when I say it was not mine either at first!

Chapters

Where Do I Start?

1. Who am I?
2. Living alone
3. Finding the one
4. Marriage and all that
5. Infertile...me? You are joking, right?

The Ugly Chrysalis

6. Counselling with some booze
7. A punch up in the uterus
8. Booze — 'the shit friend'
9. IVF again...are you sure?
10. A magpie called Bert #bekind

The Butterfly

- 11. Journeying Together
- 12. The Sausage Dog Mum
- 13. Endo surgery — what, again?
- 14. Who am I now?

Where Do I Start?

It's your life, don't let anyone make you feel guilty for living it your way

Chapter 1

Who am I?

Hmm, have you ever tried to describe yourself? Jesus, it's hard, but here goes!

So, I can conclude that I am definitely sober now, I'm definitely infertile and I am most definitely a sausage dog mum. I may be a little sausage dog mad — ok I'm a lot mad, but trust me, if you've owned one of these little dogs you'd defo fall in love with their personality and be as mad as me. Sausage dogs are special in their own way and they have their own little community, but I'll tell you all about that in another chapter — just know that sausage dogs are a massive part of my life. I absolutely love all animals; in fact, I prefer them to people. People can be harsh and unkind whereas animals just love you no matter what, even if you are a complete dick sometimes.

So, my childhood years were pretty good. I remember there were many good times. Dad worked his butt off to jet us all round the world and Mum sacrificed her working life to look after us morons at home. We had a beautiful family home in Surrey (quite affluent darling what, what, what). Mum and Dad were into water skiing and we had a great childhood learning how to water-ski and having fun with our jet boat on a private lake in Reading with two other families we mingled with. And yes, we always went to the pub on the way home from the lake, although I wasn't drinking at this point as my parents would probably have gotten in trouble.

An Orangina and a packet of cheese and onion crisps were all I looked forward to — oh, and the pub had to have swings and slides otherwise there wasn't much point in stopping at that pub. Can't say that point bothered me in later years and as life went on, I kinda wish I still liked Orangina and cheese and onion crisps instead!

Oh yes, and I am now 33 years old. Oh, and my husband has chimed in, something about the wrong age, hold on...What's that, darling? You're 37, not 33... I am not that old, how dare you! Ok, hands up, I'm 30 fucking 7 (coughs). I realise this is not an old lady age but it is for my lovely egg fertility years, so in my head, I'm defo a lot younger because if you want kids, who wants to be heading towards menopause before you've had them? Hold on, slow down. Wait: I've not got one yet. My stupid body doesn't seem to have a pause button. If I was religious, I'd be having a word with him, her or it up there. I'd ask if maybe he/she thought about it in the next creation, perhaps you could modernise the female body to put a 'wait' button on for fertility so we could start it just at the right time? Sounds good to me — perfect, cheers, nice one (thumbs up).

Ok so let's start with school; I was excellent at art (grade A) and not too bad at geography and design technology, but hated everything else. It was all complete shit (ok I was just bad at it). Christ, maths was the absolute worst (apologies to all the maths lovers). I'm sorry but whoever thought teaching me algebra was going to help me work out my credit card bill and real-life stuff is an idiot; it didn't tell me if I could buy that really expensive handbag or not, did it? No!

Anyway, let's not rant about horrible maths, all you ever need to know is — if there isn't a minus number in your account then you are good to go shopping or to the pub. Yes, I was in the bottom class at maths but who cares? I'm doing pretty well now, so bugger ya maths classes!

I didn't do too bad in my GCSEs, I got mainly Cs, one A and a B, which was good enough to go to college to piss about some more before I had to actually get a real job. On to Guildford College GNVQ advanced in Leisure and Tourism here we come. Now the only reason I took this course was because I thought I'd have half a chance of becoming an air hostess and jetting off around the world — see ya later suckers! I trot along to a Virgin open day having almost completed my course, only to realise I'm one bloody inch too short — fuck! What the hell am I gonna do now? Oh, bollocks, I'll have to look for a job whilst I work it out… get the paper out… hmmm, how about a junior admin assistant for a solicitor's office in Guildford? Ok, sounds good: let's roll with that.

Roll on a good few years later, a few courses and a few jobs later, having stuck in the legal field, I ended up being a legal secretary for about 13/14 years (yawn). I worked in medical negligence, personal injury, road traffic accidents, commercial conveyancing and residential conveyancing (yawn, am I right?). I decided to quit that career in September 2019 (woohoo!).

I currently live in a quiet, quaint countryside village in Hampshire in a four-bed detached house (yes I'm not doing too bad) and I love it. It took us eight years to get the dream house, but just because you've got a beautiful house doesn't mean you have a beautiful life. No one should judge anyone based on what they see, because you have no idea what each person is struggling with. What's that saying people use? Don't judge a book by its cover — damn right (although my cover doesn't look too bad).

You may have guessed from reading the back of my book that I don't drink now, although I damn well used to. In fact, I'm not sure what else I actually did other than drink, but I'll explain more as we go on. So instead of drinking, I do 'other' things now. You seem to find things you never used to do when you give up drinking. For instance, I'm writing this book; I also write to a chap on death row in the USA — yes I know, it's not for everyone but he is a human being at the end of the day and in my eyes, everyone deserves a friend in this world without judgment and writing to him has given me the confidence to actually write this book.

I'm not sure I'm even good at writing but I'm giving it a go because I haven't really got anything to lose. I'm not doing this for financial gain as you will learn, I'm doing it in the vague hope it reaches people who may be going or have gone through a similar struggle and to put a smile on their face; to let them know they are not alone in this crazy world. For me it's about getting people to not judge others and be kind, that's the goal.

Some other useless information about me is I absolutely love watching stuff about ghosts and the supernatural world; yes, I'm one of those people who believe in something else and I like to think that the little robin who pops down now and then is a lost loved one. I don't think it's a bad thing to believe in something, some people believe in one God, and also many different gods, I'm sure some people believe in fairies but I've learnt not to judge people because if it gives them inner peace, then what's the harm? As long as they're not forcing their beliefs on you it doesn't matter plus it's good not to be narrow-minded.

So, talking of not judging, I also like watching documentaries about murders and prisoners — innocent until proven guilty and all that, although America's justice system seems crazy to me, we won't go there. I love horse riding but sadly the stables near me are shut; maybe the horse heard about my fat arse, ha-ha. Oh, I read lots of self-help books, I've got a lot of books on being sober, mindfulness and fertility, but I do like the odd chick flick book.

Among other things, I love to make bracelets; I'm not that great at it and you probably can't see from my terrible pic that I like to add a butterfly on each bracelet, but they are there because I feel that after everything I've gone through and currently going through, I'm now turning into a beautiful (ok, maybe a little too far) butterfly.

I guess you could say I'm a creative person; I love to do paint by numbers and paint by diamond pictures…yes, I know they're cheating but who cares? It makes me feel good. Besides I've tried drawing and painting and for some reason, I'm not as good as I was in school, I guess practice makes perfect but paint by numbers is so much easier. I also run my own business and my own support group but there's more on that in the coming chapters.

In a nutshell, I guess I'm mostly an easy-going, happy-ish, kind, caring, stubborn people-pleaser type of woman who has got through some difficulties in life and I'm now slowly building that massive bridge to get over to the other side…might paint it pink just for fun. I can see it seems to be shinning a bright happy light over the other side and I'm doing a casual stroll towards it, so I invite you to join me for the stroll, as it's nice to have friends along the way… and sausage dogs obviously, definitely bring your dog. I've bought mine, Millingtons Moomin. Ok her name is Millie Moo, I just like to call her lots of silly names. She's on the next page so please do boop her nose, she's extremely friendly. She's my trusty sidekick and best friend in the whole world and I'm not too sure how or who I would be without her.

It's probably my maternal instinct that I've never had the chance to use, cause this goddam world is cruel sometimes but more about that in another chapter. If you want to learn more about me then you've gotta read on…

Millie Moo

PS — The picture quality throughout the book isn't the best due to my bad photography skills, but you get the idea!

Chapter 2
Living Alone

So, living alone has its benefits but you also do get kinda lonely and stuck in your own head. I have analysed my life over the years and all I can come up with is that my drinking stemmed right back from my family breakup — they do say it's usually trauma and I can conclude that nothing else happened before that, so it must be that. Yes, I'm aware that this is a very common thing these days, you're lucky if your parents are still together — in fact, it's a miracle! I guess too many Disney films and growing up with the perfect family life rendered me safe from that one thing no kid wants to happen and when it did happen, it was like nothing I ever experienced. Family breakdown right before my eyes; nothing would be the same again. I didn't want to live a different life, I liked the one we had. I didn't want to move to a new house and I hated that we wouldn't all be together ever again.

I lived with my mum and sister in Guildford throughout my GCSE years at school and we only saw our dad on Wednesdays and every other weekend. That totally sucked, going from seeing dad every day to a schedule, but that's what it was. Mum did her best to keep us happy and looked after us.

A few years later, I ended up moving out and living on my own because I couldn't face being around any heartache that came from the family breakup, plus three women under one roof, it's not heaven on earth. There is no blame here, it's life and it happened but how I dealt with it wasn't the best way.

I'm now all grown up and I can appreciate how staying together in a relationship while you don't get on and despite having children, can be really detrimental to your mental health. I guess one door closes and another door opens but you don't really understand all this until you get older and have had relationships yourself. At the time, you just want your perfect family childhood to continue. Strangely, most of my dreams are now located in my childhood bedroom looking out the window, creeps me out but in a way, it's kinda comforting that my memory hasn't forgotten my childhood.

So living alone, it's official, I'm a weekend alcoholic or 'binge drinker' as commonly referred to. Oh, hold on, it just went into Thursday is the new Friday and hold on… yep it's also Friday is the new Saturday. Ok but what about Wednesday? We can't miss out hump day! Ok then, let's make that a reason to celebrate as well then. We have to have one day off a week so let's go for Tuesday. That leaves Monday and I don't know about you but I do feel that after a Monday, one needs a drink or several to get over the Monday work blues. Yeah sure, why not? Oh, Jesus, I'm drinking most days, can you be a full-time binge drinker? Ok don't panic, it's fine, most 23/24-year olds do this anyway, so what's the big deal?

I'm gonna guess that having not dealt with the family 'trauma,' I just tucked it deep down inside and hid all the emotion of it all plus having discovered this amazing drug called alcohol helps massively at keeping it all hidden.

That's it, throw away the key, pick up a vino and keep picking up vinos... ok you can stop now. Nope, I can't, it's impossible; the wine monster has got me. The next picture is me all over, what can I say?

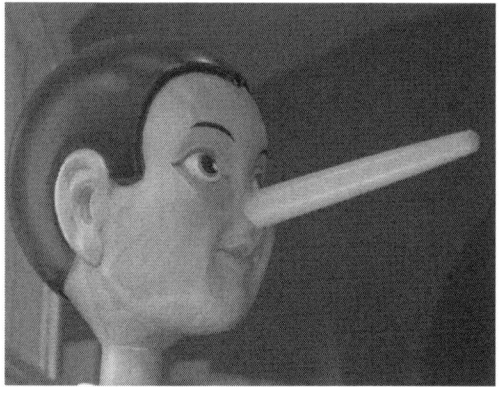

Me when I tell myself I'm not going to drink this weekend.

I absolutely loved my life when I lived in Guildford. I could go out when I wanted and see who I wanted and it was my first taste of proper freedom. It took a while for it to wear thin and realise I don't have any money left. So obviously, I got a roommate; meet Pickles, my trusty hamster below. She lived with me for two years before she sadly died in my hands, that was a sad time. A drink was needed for that night.

Pickles! The little fatty

I'm now about 23/24 years old and I live in my own separate room in a four-bed house with other housemates in the centre of Guildford. All my friends live down the road and my legal secretary job is a ten-minute walk from my house — oh yes, I've hit the jackpot for walking (staggering) home after a good night out — winner.

My housemates are awesome — well two of them are — the other one well she is, how can I put it? Inconsiderate! Luckily, she stays in her room a lot. So, James and Nick are about my age and they're both quality blokes and... hold on a bloody minute... hell yes, they LOVE beer. This is definitely the room to rent in this house! Things are turning out alright.

Nick and James spent many a night in the sitting room watching Top Gear and drinking beer after beer, so much so that they made a beer table — yes, a 'coffee' table made of used beer cans. It was pure quality but unfortunately, it made the house smell like a pub so we couldn't keep it for too long. I can proudly say, I did help somewhat with this achievement, surely it's one to put on the CV?

The legendary beer table.

Oh yes, this is the beast. I totally expected furniture stores to be selling these in the future... not sure why this didn't take off, it's legendary.

Nick also had a friend called Kenny, who came round quite a lot to drink with us. Nick had worn his trousers so much that they started to split so Kenny decided to make a beer tent out of them. Trust me, this was quite amusing when you're drunk. Nick was a bit like a loveable teenager (if there's such a thing), he didn't see his parents much so I sort of looked after him a bit, but he was never a great cook. His space in the freezer consisted of chips and chicken nuggets and if you eat too much of this without vegetables, as Nick found out, you get bum AIDS (well that's what we rudely called it, so please don't be offended) it's actually haemorrhoids or grapes hanging out ya bum. So, amusingly, Nick couldn't sit down at work and his job entailed sitting down serving the bank customers… I'm mean and I laughed a lot, he got a lot of daily texts. "Are you sitting down for this Nick?" Hahaha!

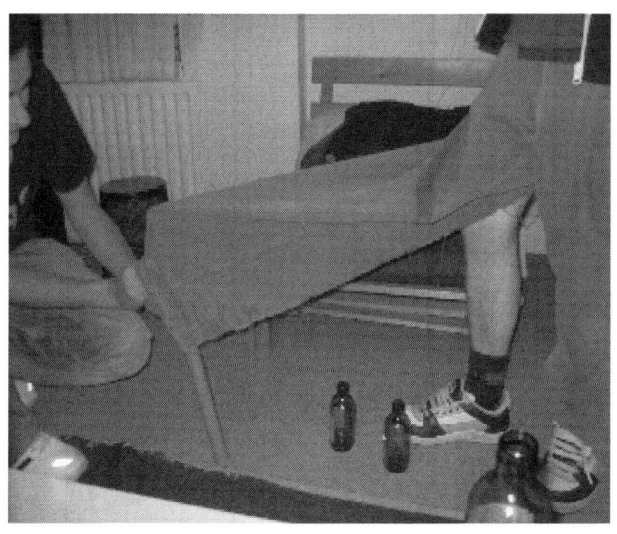

Nick's beer tent trousers.

Nick, James and I used to do a weekly shop at Tesco in Guildford. This was always amusing as one of us would often go down the medication aisle and pick up something you didn't want in your trolly and throw it in when you're not looking then calmly and loudly say, when you're at the till: "I put that Vagisil in you wanted," or "I've shoved that anisole in that you needed…" the irony is Nick actually needed it in the end ha-ha.

Me and Nick – yes, drunk.

Our other housemate was a girl who lived in a room which was actually the attic. She probably still lives there but she was quite lazy with washing up. If you've ever lived with random people, the polite thing to do is clean and wash up after yourself, not leave it for anyone else, you don't live with your mum anymore! She was well known for using all of the plates and cutlery and not washing up. One day I got so fed up with this that I washed up enough plates and cutlery for Nick, James and I and I then put the remainder in the washing up bowl and left it outside her room. I can kinda remember she wasn't very happy, but I didn't really care, cause I wasn't happy either. A few months after James and I had moved out of the house, Nick told me he got even more fed up and put all the plates and cutlery in a black sack so there was nothing for her to use — ha-ha, bloody legend.

Aww, we love Nick, he cracks me up that boy. He would say every morning without fail, "I hate my job I don't want to go to work, I want to quit," and in the end he did. He left 'cause he got a job on a Disney cruise ship as a bass player, he met a girl in Canada and got married and now lives there. We still keep in contact to this day… his dreams came true!

Back to the drinking. I'm pretty sure most of you know what it's like having a hangover at work. You just can't be bothered to do anything much, so you do the bare minimum, have lots of tea and oh yes — must get a sausage sarnie on the walk up to work. Hold on… I have to sit down, feel really ill, dizzy. Ok, ok I'm fine, not going to be sick.

I held down my job, although I was caught asleep under my desk (yes, asleep) on one occasion. The thing is I'd been doing it for quite a while, but no one seemed to notice. My boss at the time hauled me into her office and asked if there was anything she could help me with and suggested I should see a doctor. Yikes, I felt really bad about it for a while but I just changed my carb-loaded hangover breakfast and lunch for cereal and salad instead and that seemed to work — phew got away with that one! Plus, the alcohol gunt (stomach) is a bit flatter- winner.

I'm sure we all reminisce about back in the day with our friends now we're a bit older. I still speak to, and on the odd occasion, go out with my friends that used to be our big going out drinking group. There wasn't a weekend where we didn't go into Guildford town, but not before predrinking at mine (of course). My Bessie mate, Leila, would rush down to mine straight from her job on a Friday night in her little yellow Fiat Punto driving like an arse with her dodgy number plate (ha-ha, love ya, buddy). She'd park across the road from my house, I'd see her from my window, overnight bag in one hand and two bottles of vino in the other — fuck yes, the weekend had begun!

Pic of my bud on next page — not even a glass, we were so classy!

Go on Leila, get it down ya neck girl!

I was no longer alone when my friends were around me and we partied until the early hours of the morning, it was great. We went to a well known pub chain to get a few cheap ones in and hope that we meet blokes who would buy us a drink or two, which seemed to work, then we'd go halves on a cheap bottle of vino in every pub. Not one for wanting the party to ever end, we'd inevitably end up at a club called 'The Drink,' but you had to be there before 10 pm to get in the queue with all the other drunks. Pay your £5 to get in then hang around the bar until someone offered to buy you a drink — winner — continue doing amazing dance moves (or so I thought) on the disgusting sticky floor and then stagger home about 3 or 4 am. Good job I only live ten minutes away!

Well, it was all fun until the hangover kicked in that morning. Oh, my days! Why did I go out again? Why couldn't I be sensible and have a pizza and DVD night with my mates and get an early night? Nope, my stupid alcohol shit friend wanted to not just go out, she wanted to go *out out*, but not just for a few hours — oh no, it had to be most of the night and god knows how I made it home but I somehow did. I also managed to have a full shower and get into my PJs! WTF, who does that when they're drunk?

I dreaded when the time came for Leila to go home on a Sunday cause that would mean I'd be alone again with my thoughts and demons...no, don't go Leila! Ok, I must find another friend to pop out with on Sundays just for a swift one or two, ok three, but don't tell anyone.

I had one long-term relationship when I was in college and he was (so I thought) the love of my life until he got involved with some nasty people which I didn't know at the time and so he split up with me. I didn't get any explanation, he just dumped me and ignored me. I guess that sparked me not to trust that any man would love me from then on (oh no another trauma, for Christ's sake can we not do this again). Sadly, I didn't really have a boyfriend when I was in my early 20s, more like I had boys who messed me about, which messed my head and heart up and so that made me want to hit the booze some more. My family had split up, I was living alone (own choice) and now boys are messing my head up with me thinking they actually like me but no, they were just using me. Ta, thanks for that! Life wasn't quite turning out how I imagined it.

It's okay I'm only in my 20s, plenty of time. I'm turning 24, I've got a month's worth of weekend fun — don't ask me why I didn't wait until I was 25 — I just wanted to have a month of celebrations, the May birthday month of fun. Can't ruddy wait. So one weekend was for family celebrations, one weekend was for my usual drinking crowd out on the town, one weekend was for friends who weren't in that group and the last weekend was a free-for-all BBQ party at mine — holy cow, why did I do that? It was not a classy affair as you can tell by the potato wine and the party hat.

40

Obviously, my Bessie mate Leila made me a penis cake! Well, we had to keep the classy affair up, why wouldn't you? Sadly, someone decided it would be a really good idea to throw the cake (in their drunken state) over my neighbour's fence. Yes, they were a bunch of student willies but they defo didn't require my lovingly made cake. They were students who rented next door and they were always annoying me with their late-night party noises.

Our party definitely got out of hand when ketchup started being squirted over the walls. I believe I passed out upstairs having not had my usual shower or got into my PJs — defo a heavy drinking night.

This lifestyle pattern continued for as long as I can remember until I found 'the one.'

Chapter 3
Finding The One

Ok, so you know about my college love, which ended — it probably wasn't love, just one of those 'relationships' you have in college. Well, I'm now about to turn 25 so it's 2008, and yet again planning an epic night out — full of booze obviously.

Out to Five and Lime in Guildford we go, it's a bar full of pretentious stuck up people who think they're all better than everyone else. So yeah, lets head there cause it's got a lovely outside area with a DJ and I might find some nice boyfriend material, even though I'm definitely not stuck up, and I'm pretty sure I'm not much of a lady; it probably doesn't help living with two larger lout housemates. I'm more of a functioning drunk.

Yes, this is a headless shot of me in that bar with... you guessed it... none other than a drink and some terrible extensions. Looks like a vodka Redbull-puke!

The night continues and we, as usual, end up in that club 'The Drink' at the bottom of town and apparently, my future husband was around for the night as he was a friend of one of the group but I never actually met him that night.

A few days after my hangover, I was on Messenger in my room (yes Messenger back in them days!) and a chap called Simon popped up wanting to be my friend. I had no idea who he was but what the hell? I accepted him. He was actually over one of my friends' houses and had got hold of my messenger details, it was slightly creepy but anyway, we started talking quite a lot. He came out on a few nights where he bought me a lot of drinks and supplied me with a lot of fags — jackpot — and yes, I smoked back then (yuck).

It's the end of May 2008... fuck it, let's go on a girl's holiday with the besties to Zante, most of which I can't remember. Hmmm, that might be my trusty shit friend Mr Alcohol's fault, I really must be having a word. Thank god for the pictures that documented the holiday; it looked epic I must say.

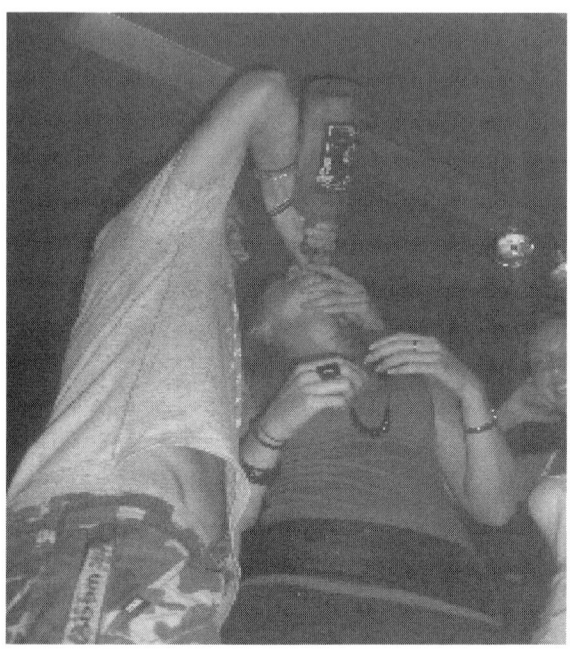

Me getting a free drink at a bar in Zante... who'd have thought it? It definitely wasn't a cup of tea. The picture quality is not the best, we didn't have iPhone quality cameras back in those days.

Oh yes, me having a fag and drinking out of a fishbowl on a bar in Zante….you seeing a trending pattern? Oh and I'm quite skinny…I guess life happened after that!

When I got home from Zante, after a few more sessions talking to Simon on Messenger, we met up a few times and he asked me to be his girlfriend one night when he stayed over at mine. He seemed like a quiet boy who lived with his parents and certainly didn't have a problem with alcohol. He drove his Honda Civic Type R around like a rude boy and always had his silver chain on – I loved it, someone half-decent was interested in me! I obviously accepted this gesture and after a month or so of dating, he told me he loved me when we were sitting in a well known cheap bar (classy) one evening and I said it back; finally, my fairy tale life was beginning. I did think this is a joke; how can he love me? I don't have anything interesting about me, all I do is drink. Meh, what the hell, just go with it.

Anyway, after a few more months, he asked me to move into his parents with him as it seemed stupid for me to pay out £500 ($671) a month to rent a room next door to annoying loud students and we could start saving for our first house. So, I did, but I didn't realise how much of a lifestyle change I was going to have. I was so used to coming and going when I liked, cooking and washing for myself, that moving back to a parent's house certainly had an impact on me.

I had friends texting me all the time wondering if I was about to go out for a drink but suddenly, I found I couldn't just go out; I had a boyfriend and I lived elsewhere now. This hit me hard and I went into a depressive state where, for some reason, I couldn't quite believe this boy loved me and wanted me and I couldn't just pop out on my own anymore… ahhhh I was stuck between a rock and a hard place and I just couldn't trust anything and so I was angry and cried a lot of the time confused about life and what I should do and I wanted to run away and drink.

I had to have constant reassurance that Simon loved me; there were some dark times where I actually wanted to end my life because I couldn't understand who would want to be with someone whose life revolved around drinking. Sadly, I felt like I lost everything again, just like I did when my family split up. I stopped seeing friends as much and I moved out (my choice) of my rented house. It was really hard to adjust yet again, but this wasn't Simon's fault at all; he was doing all he could to make my life better but I just couldn't see it and so I had to seek help from a doctor and I was put on antidepressants. Bloody depression. Someone said to me once that depression is thinking about the past and anxiety is worrying about the future, how true that is!

We did have some amusing times, don't get me wrong. I bought a black Audi TT, my first ever sports car, and to be honest, it was quite a jump up from my battered green ancient Peugeot 306 thing but, as with most things in my life it was tainted. The first drive home after I purchased it, the ruddy engine warning light came on — for Christ's sake, really? A few months of Audi ownership passed and I, for some reason, thought it would be a good idea to park it on the wall! Thank god for my dad who was a crash repair specialist at the time. Then the TT finally broke down on me a few months after that. Luckily, I was on an estate and not the main road, but that cost me a hefty sum and after that I said goodbye and I've not owned another Audi since!

Here is the tainted beast.

We didn't go on many holidays as we were saving for a house, we only went on one to Ibiza but I was drunk for most of that. We did, however, go on a short (a very short) camping trip, we bought a stupidly big tent (as you do) and went to a campsite in lovely Brighton. I can't remember much. I can tell you, however, we got there quite late in the day because everyone there had their tents up and they were enjoying the countryside air. They now had some entertainment in watching us struggle to put a tent up that was big enough for a family of four, which we'd never done before, and we probably looked like we were drunk doing it.

Well about an hour or so later, I defo needed a drink. Luckily, we bought red wine because that doesn't need chilling — winner. We had a blow-up bed and our own pillows and blanket, so it was like a proper bed inside the tent. We had some shit food cooked by us on a tiny camping stove and then proceeded to neck the vino, whilst smoking of course. My 15/20 a day habit turned into at least 30/40 an evening habit when I was drinking. Ummm, no other words other than 'yuck' — oh, my poor lungs!

The evening continued with the couple in the tent opposite inviting over to sit outside their tent. Honestly, I couldn't tell you what was said, there was a lot of wine and fags consumed. I do, however, remember running out of cigs and trying to fashion one out of the ones I'd already smoked because I was desperate — Jesus that's disgusting.

Well after the night ended, I decided to pass out fully clothed in the 'bed' area, and a few hours later, hello red wine and crap sausages – yes, I chundered it all up! Proper lush. So, we decided it might be a good idea if we just pack up everything before the whole site wakes up and leave plus throw away what I'd ruined in the campsite bin. That was pure class and the world's shortest holiday trophy goes to me. The tent stayed in the garage for some years until we chucked it out, vowing never to go camping again. Since then, we've stuck to camping in static caravans, much easier and there is a proper bog to puke in, should the need occur, plus I don't have to look like a nutty drunk trying to erect a bloody tent.

We had a lot of arguments and adjustments on my part to get through over the next year dealing with the drinking and depression and my self-worth was at an all-time low, but we made it through and went to look at houses. We scoped out the field across the road from the house we had put an offer on and in the distance, there was an enormous 20 stone man with a tiny pup on a lead… well that didn't look odd at all! Ha-ha. Me being me, I bounded over to find out what this pup was, I could see it was tiny and long. Sure enough, it was a sausage dog called Dolly and I immediately fell in love and had to have one. As soon as we exchanged on our house, we found a breeder in Kent and went to see our pup but couldn't pick her up for nine weeks… omg that bit killed me — nine bloody weeks!

We bought our first two bed one-bathroom house with a garden and parking for £212,500 ($289,496) on Goldsworth Park in 2010. Oh my god, epic moment on the day of completion, I got back home early from work, packed up my car and then Simon's mum came out and said, "Do you know where you're going?" I replied, "Umm nope, no idea!" Ha-ha, what a wally! I was so excited I forgot I didn't know where the house was as Goldsworth Park is a bit of a rabbit warren, so Jackie came with me.

So here it is; such a cute, cosy house and we loved it. Crack the Prosecco open… oh crap, we're living on our own now, there are no rules and a huge American style fridge to store booze in. What could possibly go wrong?

So here it is, the world's smallest kitchen with the biggest fridge — cheers.

I changed jobs to be a legal secretary in Woking town centre so I was only a bus ride away, so there was no point parking in town. £80 ($107) a month bus wanker ticket versus £2,000 ($2686) a year parking in town, it's a no brainer! A couple who worked with me also lived around the corner and, luckily for me, loved a drink or ten. There were lots of work nights out getting drunk, I don't think I did anything embarrassing for once. I just got obscenely drunk and ate a lot of kebabs — standard then!

Chapter 4
Marriage and all that

We picked up our first ever puppy together the day we moved in. Yes, the day we moved in! We left our parents unpacking our house whilst we popped down to Kent to pick up our reserved first baby puppy. She was nine weeks old and the most adorable thing ever! Here she is, she was called Bunty but we renamed her Poppy… or Poppy Pop Pops, Poparge Woo Waa Ding Dees, Pop Pops. Yes, some silly names but our baby and totally adorable.

We all lived in this perfect little two-bed house for approximately four years, we had some major readjusting to each other now that we were actually running our own house, and believe me, that caused some arguments. Who cleaned the bathroom last? Who emptied the dishwasher last? Who hoovered last? Christ, I need a drink already, can we just be a team? Or we could move back to Simon's parents — no, no we must just get through this and manage to live together, we'd just done that for two years with his parents so we just need to learn how this system works a bit better on our own together. First things first, let's crack open the wine before I get my duster out.

I discovered I could hide my drinking when we lived at Simon's parents; I was young and it's clearly classed as acceptable to get completely off your face on booze most weekends when you're in your early twenties so no one ever said anything and quite clearly I thought it was acceptable as well.

Obviously, we would have booze whilst watching a film in our bedroom at Simon's parents, but I got the drunkest at weekends out on the town with friends so when we got our own house, well that was just a ticket to freedom on the booze front again.

When Poppy was about six months old, we decided it would be nice to get her a sister and so we went back to the same breeder and she had this little cutie pie called Hettie. We renamed her Millie Moo and here she is... one, two, three... aww.

Pop and Moo became the bestest of friends… aww, look at them!

On Christmas morning in 2012, two years after moving to our new house, Simon got up at 6 am and made a coffee. He seemed rather happy and a bit twitchy though I couldn't work out why, so I carried on with a lay-in snuggling the sausages. Yes, they came for a cuddle in bed in the morning. Who could resist, right?

Simon brings me coffee, asks me to sit up, and at this point, I'm looking like a swamp thing with morning breath — lush! He then gets down on one knee and proposes… Oh. My. God. Yes, yes, yes, I've been waiting for like five years, what took you so ruddy long?

The Christmas day continued over at Simon's parents with — you guessed it — booze and lots of it. I believe we sank approximately five bottles of Prosecco, with lots of in-between beers. We definitely celebrated. Boxing day was a lovely hangover, one I didn't enjoy, but hey ho. In true Christmas spirit, we carried on the drink fest with my mum and her partner. I'm sure there was a row in there somewhere, the usual Christmas one everyone has!

We decided to get married on my 30th birthday, on the 10 May 2013. I get double presents and he won't ever forget the date! It was a fab day and I hardly touched my food because all I wanted to do was enjoy the party and drink. Weirdly enough, I didn't get drunk at my own wedding. One, because the dress was too tight and two, because every time I put my drink down for a photo it got taken away — how rude! I'd actually say it's far better to attend a wedding than to host one because you don't have to put on a ruddy smile and speak to everyone every five seconds — exhausting. I knew I should have gone to Vegas to get married, that's ultimately what we wanted to do, but for some reason, we settled for a pub/barn down the road — everyone needs a pub or bar at a wedding, it's obligatory!

Some wedding evidence… yes, we did it!

Don't worry, we did go to Vegas, albeit two years later for our honeymoon; it was on my birthday/our wedding anniversary, but we got there and it was one of the best holidays we've had. We stayed at the MGM Grand, which was totally amazing. If you haven't been, get booking as you won't regret it. I confess, I may have got drunk in Vegas a lot but trust me, if you know about Vegas, you know it's the city that never sleeps.

We decided to do a daily 'annoyance' on Facebook to document our honeymoon holiday, it was great fun. On my birthday/our wedding evening we worked our way down the strip frequenting some bars but also picking up the odd can of beer from a corner shop which happened to be in every hotel-casino — clearly for the drunks (tick, that's me).

We had booked a meal in a posh restaurant but by the time we got there, we were quite shitfaced, from what I remember the waiter slightly frowned but we didn't care and got even drunker cause we were in Vegas baby. It's a shame I can't remember it much — this is what alcohol does to you ladies and gentlemen, it blanks your memory.

Here is some proof we did actually go!

So, back to reality and I can tell you that almost every Sunday we go to Simon's parents for a traditional Sunday lunch (yes, we still do) and I absolutely love it. It's so lovely that they all get together still and that I can be part of that; it feels like a family again and I feel safe. That didn't stop me from having several glasses of vino for Sunday lunch because who doesn't have wine when you go out for lunch?

I did start to think I'm the only one who is having a glass of wine or three every time we go there — oops. I'd make sure that Simon would be driving and I'd get a bit upset if he wanted me to drive so he always drove as Simon wasn't bothered about drinking as much as me; he could take it or leave it. I honestly don't know how he does it, I could never just have one; what's the actual point in that? Clearly you take it, not leave it.

I've grown up watching my parents have fun drinking with friends, having parties and going out to the pub a lot with friends which is not a bad thing, they were having fun, but in my mind, this was 'normal' behaviour. It seems to be the thing adults do to relax and have fun with their friends. No bugger told me you have to try and control this drinking thing, and no one told me it would be bloody hard to do that if you want to block some trauma out instead of dealing with it.

When Simon's mum tells me about his childhood and all about them, they were not like mine with the drinking and party habits when he was growing up, they were more reserved and didn't do parties or have pub fun with several families. No one is playing the blame game again here, every family has their own way of living and having fun but I'm now seeing it is quite true that you do learn off people you live with. Obviously, it's up to you if you turn into a drunk in later life.

I've always thought it's funny how most parents don't condone you smoking and tell you all about the bad things it does to you, but they don't do it for alcohol... I wonder why!? Oh yes, because it would highlight their own drinking habits.

So back to Simon and I. On most weekends we would get to Friday and binge drink the entire weekend because, although I wasn't going out with friends drinking every night, I got into a habit of having a glass of wine or beer or several most evenings when we got home from work. Weekends would be worse and I'd make sure we didn't have anything to get up for on a Saturday so I could get drunk on Friday and deal with my hangover on the Saturday in time enough to drink again Saturday night — isn't that what most people do?

I look back now and realise we didn't ever really go out and do much together because all I was consumed with doing is drinking and I thought that was my go-to fun thing to do. There was one rare night where we did go out to town but if we did go out, it had to be near to where we lived so we could get a taxi cheap and it had to involve alcohol otherwise there was no point in my book.

One evening we started in a bar, which is now closed, called Charlie Choys. It's a cocktail bar — big mistake! I wasn't used to drinking cocktails and so I had two long island iced teas — oh my god, they are potent, and oh boy, I seem to be quite drunk already. We'd decided we were going to Pizza Express to eat but I wanted to drink more so we booked the table as late as we could. We carried on drinking at a bar that was next door to Pizza Express, lots of beer this time so mixing the drinks up a bit. No problem I can handle this, I'm having fun with my husband — or so I thought, well my shit friend alcohol thought that anyway.

Nine o'clock rocks round; I am completely drunk, we go to Pizza

Express and get seated by the door on a table for two, there aren't many people in there (luckily). We order our pizza and just as the waitress walks away… Jesus, I've chundered all over the table, yep I'm definitely not feeling well. I can hear Simon being angry with me but I can't function properly, I see him go over to the counter to pay for the pizza and then he grabs me and we leave with no pizza! Oh god, I've messed up here, I'm starving, I've got puke on me and my husband is mad. This is NOT how the night was supposed to go. Plus, did I mention that I'm starving?

I can laugh about this now but trust me, at the time it was bad, it ruined the entire weekend. There were a few incidents, not quite so bad but it led Simon to decide he didn't want to 'go out' anymore with me because my drinking made him anxious. Wow, I had no idea he was angry with me and I was sad that he thought that about me but it didn't stop me from drinking because at this point I didn't think I had a problem.

It was a friend's birthday and everyone was going to Wimbledon dog racing. Well hello, that entails drinking and I knew Simon wouldn't want to go so it meant I could get extremely drunk again without him — woohoo! I lost at dog racing and man did I get pissed, luckily my friend dropped me off home but I only made it to the front door and collapsed in a pile. Simon opened the door and dragged me in but left me to sort myself out. Can't say I remember what happened after that, but Simon wasn't happy with me for the rest of that weekend again — oops.

This marriage thing is getting hard, but it can't be all down to my drinking….

yeah just ignore it, keep drinking luv. Um, ok then.

In April 2014 we moved to a detached house — yes detached, wow-wee, with a garage and a conservatory, but it's all in the aid of securing a home for a family to come like people do when they get married. That's what society expects you to do.

Yep, we're moving up in the house world… wait for it, there is a downside. I mean it was a good stepping stone but we were near the worst pub in history and near the private airport (not commercial luckily). The best bit was we had lovely neighbours surrounding us, one of which I still keep in touch with, so it wasn't all bad. Oh, plus I moved jobs again, yes, a legal secretary but for a firm that was literally ten mins drive away, if that.

Well, what can I tell you other than we had quite a few parties at this house. We decided to buy a lazy spa — best purchase ever, we used it a lot, the good thing is I never chundered in it, so it was a good reusable purchase.

Here is the bad boy lazy spa in all its glory.

Here is a terrible drunk picture of us in it.

I can't actually tell you how many hot tub BBQ parties we had because I've lost count. It wasn't all bad, we did have some epic times but looking back on it now I can see that we were both riddled with grief and sadness and trying our best to portray a happy child-free lifestyle. A sort of we-don't-care attitude. There is only so long you can keep this up my friends before you crack!

Chapter 5
Infertile...me! You are joking?

Well, cue the usual conversation with friends and family after you've been married for a while or when you get a puppy… "Oh, it will be kids next!" Yeah ok sure, because that happens for everyone on this planet normally (rolls eyes). I guess that's the trouble with society; we're conditioned from a young age with baby dolls and we play mummies and daddies so we grow up thinking we will have the perfect family, just like the one we grew up knowing — well most of us. Hold on, this story for me is, "Sorry love, I hate to tell you this but it's not going to happen." Fuck, really?

So, about a year before we got married, we were 'trying' for a baby, I didn't think anything of the fact we didn't fall because we had only been trying six months and then we had the stress of the wedding so we carried on as normal. Sadly, I kept having bleeding episodes after intercourse but again, I didn't think much of it. I'd already had a smear test which, if you don't know yet, is the test that every woman is invited to have performed every three years from the age of 25. It detects cancerous or 'abnormal' cells that could develop into cancer if not treated; Jade Goody comes to mind so please, please ladies get yourself tested! It doesn't hurt and saves lives. So, my test came back as an abnormal result — God's sake! I then had to have a colposcopy laser treatment... all I can say is ouch! Holy cow, I did not enjoy that. I had no idea this would be one of many ouchy horrible treatments to come, and I may as well have just never bought any more nice pants because I'll have them down so often, they won't get used.

In the meantime, we had both been to the doctor to get our fertility checked out and we were both 'fine,' they couldn't give us any explanation as to why we couldn't conceive so the usual go-to conversation of "just keep trying and relax, I'm sure it will happen," was told to us. Cheers for that useless statement.

The next stage was to send me to have my fallopian tubes cleaned out just in case I had any blockages. Well, that was another unpleasant procedure, although not painful just uncomfortable. After that, we were told to carry on as normal for six months before they would consider putting us forward for National Health Service (NHS) In Vitro Fertilisation (IVF). Yep, I'm still drinking my 'normal' amount of booze. I mean all these horrible treatments, and everyone telling me to relax means I deserve a reward of wine and beer to chill out with surely? There wasn't any way I was going to be giving that up just yet, this process is far too stressful.

You can probably guess by now that the tube clear out didn't work, there was no bun in the oven, sad times. My god, I can tell you all these appointments take a toll on you especially when every month you hope to god that period doesn't come, and every time it does, you end up having a conversation in your bathroom with your period because all this stress sends you completely mad. The conversation goes something like this: "Oh great it's you again, thanks for joining the party." Period: "No worries, here to ruin your month like always so don't be mean to me!" Me: "Seriously? Can't you just bugger off and be a baby instead?" Period: "No I like to upset you, that's what I'm here for. You're welcome."

The period coming again is like a blow to your heart and your stomach; it's an emotional rollercoaster you can't get off and if you monitor your emotions, you would clearly see the big dipper every month. I have to keep on telling myself, "Enough of that negative talk woman, come on, keep calm and carry on."

On to the gruelling IVF — oh boy, what a whirlwind of a rollercoaster trip the first time was. So initially it took some time to get 'approved' for NHS IVF. You can't be over 35, can't have had any children from a previous relationship and neither can he, you can't be overweight… the list goes on. The worst bit is they send you to the maternity — yes the maternity ward — to go and have all of your tests for approval of IVF. This was the moment I realised that my world was completely different from the majority of my age group; it was like the world was moving in slow motion as I sat in the waiting room. All I could see is mounds of pregnant happy women with their partners waiting to have their scans and some with toddlers. Oh, Jesus please, please get me out of here. How awfully cruel to stick me with people who already have their little dream bundles. In my head, the receptionist said, "Hello love, sit in here and make ya self-comfortable, and whilst you're at it think about your own shit life that didn't turn out like all these people." She didn't say that, she was lovely.

By now, most of my friend group are happily pregnant or had a baby and I'm kinda falling by the wayside not really fitting in anymore. It's an awful feeling to realise that once you were all the same, going out getting drunk without a care in the world and then boom, here is your ticket madam. Oh no, hold on, you don't get one cause you're not part of the VIP club. In fact, every month you get the VIP ticket ripped out of your hand.

At this point it has crossed my mind that everyone is doing the baby thing because it's the normal route to go down and I do wonder if anyone has ever thought – wait a minute – I could have an equally amazing life without kids, but if you ask the ones with children already, believe me, it's not something they've thought about. I guess in this society you are thought of as an outsider and a bit of a weirdo if you don't like or want kids. I'd never thought about a life without kids like most; I've always wanted them and ever since my beautiful baby sausage dogs came on the scene. I knew then that I would make a great mum because if I can love something that isn't my own flesh and blood this much, imagine the love I'd have for my own.

This section of my life is a bit of a blur because it was quite a long time ago and, like I said at the beginning, it's not my cup of tea!

We did eventually, after a year or so, get approved for IVF on the NHS but here is the snag: I was only allowed one fresh round and one frozen round. I'd just moved from Surrey to Hampshire and apparently (at the time) in Surrey you could get three fresh rounds of IVF on the NHS…

what?! disappointed was not the word (this may have changed by now). I hadn't realised about this lottery postcode (ZIP code for my American friends) as it's not something that is well shouted about. Oh well, nothing I can do about that now, I just have to get on with it and so with the highest of hopes, (because no one gave me the low down properly), we pursued the IVF route.

I can tell you that you're filled with complete joy and happiness as you embark on your first round of IVF. I did mine at a clinic in Woking and walking up the stairs for the first time was crazy. All the pictures of babies on the walls gives you the hope that this is definitely going to work. Why wouldn't it? Look at all these happy couples and babies. The doctor tells me I've got a 65% chance, which in my head, is way more than 50% so it's bound to work.

We go through a huge amount of paperwork and both have a blood test; he has a sperm test and I have an internal scan. All good on his front, but I apparently have a low ovarian reserve, meaning I'm way nearer menopause then I want to be, so the doctor tells me it's a good job I'm here as I would struggle to conceive on my own, they put me on what's called a long protocol IVF route.

The nurse takes me through how to administer the hormone drugs and explains the schedule of when I'm to take them. Oh, Christ, my head is all over the place; this looks complicated, thank god my husband is here to take it in as well!

I'm issued with a bag of drugs, needles, a needle box and the journey begins. I get home and cover my table with all my drugs; I put the drugs that needed to stay at a certain temperature in the fridge — holy cow there are a lot and all of this is going inside me! Tomorrow the gruelling regime starts. The crux of the drugs is that they take over your cycle so the clinic can time it exactly right for the egg retrieval procedure.

The needle isn't too long and it's quite thin but still, I've got to inject myself, in my stomach and plunge this gunk inside me. It doesn't sound that bad but trust me when you've got to do it yourself, it's a little scary.

First of all, I have to learn how to be a chemist and suck up the exact amount of drug into the syringe without any bubbles; it's easier said than done, it took a few tries! Ok, I'm ready to plunge this bad boy into my stomach — oh god I can't do it… breath. Ok, ok, ok go. You have to release the drugs slowly which for me, I could feel it going in and that was more painful than the ruddy needle. Woo hoo, I did it! So glad the first one is over, but this has to be done twice a day for two weeks.

In between these lovely self-stabbing sessions, there were weekly clinic visits for blood tests and internal exams, basically to check if your eggs are juicy enough to come out yet. I'm looking like a lovely pincushion with all these stab marks. To ease the pain of doing it so often, I took to numbing my stomach area with an ice pack before plunging the needle in and I have to say, it may be psychological but it was a bit easier to stick a needle in.

I'd also like to inform you that your entire life is on hold whilst you're doing all these drugs and tests. You can't just pop off for a weekend away or a week holiday away, you've got to be near the clinic in case anything should go wrong. So out goes any lust, love, friendships, family time… basically any sort of life. You're a slave to IVF for a few months now.

For instance, I accidentally knocked over the liquid drug and had a panic attack… oh my god I've not got enough, what am I going to do? Ah, it's a weekend they aren't open. Husband calmed me down (bear in mind I'm a crazy hormonal pumped up bitch at the moment). The clinic had an emergency number and I was allowed to pop in to get more drugs — phew, dilemma over! (still a crazy hormonal bitch, though).

As soon as you have a scan where they say "right, I think we are about there now so you will need to take the last injection on blah blah date" for me the excitement started- oh blimey almost at operation egg removal time. When you're doing this for the first time, you don't think that this isn't going to work, you are just going along with each day and stage of the process and in the hands of doctors who are confident and never put any doubt in your mind.

There isn't any guidance for emotions on this journey you have to navigate the process yourself, mentally, and I can tell you that that side of it is extremely difficult, basically because unless you are going through it, no one will understand your feelings or anything about the process so yeah heads up here — get used to going through this whole process on your own!

Another annoying process to deal with on top of everything else is telling your boss about your treatment, appointments and having colleagues look at you when you keep nipping out once or twice a week wondering what's going on, it's hard to keep it a secret. It's not very easy to juggle appointments with work and having to make time up because of your appointments. Christ, as if this process isn't stressful enough. I defo need a hair colour appointment, I seem to have gone very grey due to the bloody stress!

I'd decided on my first IVF round to involve my family and let them know what we were doing but in hindsight, I wish I hadn't. That sounds mean but let's face it, you don't tell your family when you're gonna be having sex and trying to conceive naturally do you? Well this process, although horribly mechanical, is you trying to conceive, so it is a personal experience.

All that I wish is that the clinic had given us some degree of counselling beforehand and during the process with family because, although it is difficult to keep this to yourself, it can become very frustrating when you have family (with all good intentions) wanting to know what's going on and what's happening next, when you don't really know yourself and you're an emotional wreck.

If you're going to involve family, I would suggest having a sit-down conversation, even a counselling session or two, so they can better understand how you're feeling and learn about the process to be able to support you better and not say too much of nothing or the wrong things because they will do. I wish I'd done this!

Let's face it, every family is different, but a lot of people, if your IVF doesn't work, will just say, "Oh well I'm sure you can try again." Umm yeah, let me just get my endless money tree out of storage to pay for future rounds!

You have to be prepared for these responses because it can feel like they're just dismissing your months of physical and emotional work just to get a baby when bloody Joe Blogs down the road only has to drop her knickers. I'm pretty sure most people don't really think about or mean what they say, but to me, who is so desperately trying to have what comes so easy to everyone else, it feels like they took a shotgun to your heart and dismissed you're hardwork.

Then the media also do a fantastic job of highlighting all those women who've had babies at 45 or older, or the miracle babies after ten rounds of IVF, or after a number of miscarriages, or highlighting the new fad diet that claims to improve fertility. It's funny how they don't comment on the actual statistics of IVF failure rate, because as far as I am aware it's a lot higher than the bloody miracle stories and all this stupid nonsense they print. You have to learn to ignore it, otherwise, it can consume you and as soon as friends and family know you're going through it, they're likely to get involved in telling you about these miracle cure things. I guess it's to try and keep your hopes up but honestly, it doesn't work for me. I have no idea about the background story of these miracle people, they don't have the same body as me; we are completely different, and every one of us is unique.

The problem is no one likes to think of a fertility problem as being unfixable so they will say "I'm sure it will happen" or "you can't give up," because it's incomprehensible to people who have kids for others not to be able to have them and they have never had to think about it; infertility isn't a disease to them, it's as if you're not trying hard enough or you've not done everything available.

The way that people and society think then becomes difficult for the person struggling with fertility to cope because no one wants to understand how to help and support them and because of this mentality in society, the struggling person eventually shuts down, blocks everyone out turns to drink / drugs / marriage breakdown / family breakdown / friend breakdowns and doesn't want to share how they feel because they realise that they just don't get the validity and sympathy that people with other (in the eyes of society) believable diseases automatically receive.

You're left to deal with this infertility alone with no support and everyone close to you can't understand why you've changed and closed off. Hmm, I wonder why??

Say you have cancer and someone says to you, "Well, you'll definitely survive because they've got all sorts of things to assist you and this woman in the paper beat it who had the same cancer as you." Hold on before you say anything like that because, for all you know, the cancer that your friend or family member has may be more aggressive than the woman's in the paper, his/hers may spread, his/hers may be bigger or smaller. Do you see where I'm coming from? You can't make suggestions based on stupid news or what you've heard; it's like you're suggesting all cancers are the same when they most certainly are not.

So, put the above in the context of infertility; the same applies. No one is the same as the next infertile person and just because IVF worked for one person, it most certainly doesn't mean it will work for another — no matter how many rounds you do or how hard you try! Instead please listen to your friend or family member about THEIR problem and don't assume their problem will be fixed by IVF or any other treatment or adoption.

Back to egg retrieval! Ok, so basically you have a different drug to take 24 hours before surgery which is the big push to get the eggs ready to come out. This is the drug stored in the fridge but it didn't feel any different from the rest; it's just the best drug as it's the end of stabbing yourself because your stomach is very swollen and sore by the end of it.

Surgery, well what can I say other than you're put out so you've no idea what's going on, which is great. Your husband (bless him) will get called into the seedy room to produce the product — pressure wank or what! You'll just spend a few hours coming round and relaxing on the bed. They then tell you how many eggs you got; sadly I only got five, the average is 10 to 15 for my age so this was quite disappointing, but she did say I had a low ovarian reserve. The embryologist then puts my eggs and my husband's sperm in a Petri dish and they have an egg and sperm party. Then you're sent home to relax for a few days, they give you a bottle of stuff to help with constipation and some pessaries to stick up ya bum day and night — lovely stuff, I'll look forward to that.

Well, bugger me... I've never experienced constipation like it, agony and 12 hours of goddam pain. I have to say it was the best poo I've had in my entire life when it happened. I didn't stop taking the constipation stuff the entire time I was using pessaries; it's a side effect that no one warned me of!

The following day, the clinic called to say that sadly two of our embryos died — bummer, it means we've only got three left. Don't panic, we've still got three eggs and they're apparently good quality which is what you want! Quality over quantity. The clinic calls you every other day to tell you how your little embryos are doing and you want them to be alive and dividing which, ours were doing, woohoo! Once they get to day five, that's the best day to either freeze them or put them back in your uterus and hope for the best. We opted to freeze two and have one put back.

So off we trot back to the clinic; they show you your embryo on the screen- aww an ickle life is beginning. Then they take about ten minutes to put it back in... oh yeah, you've got to have a half-full bladder as well. I can't say this is a comfortable procedure by any means. It felt like I was going to wee on the doc.

So, after the procedure, we went for a slap-up English breakfast down the road. We've now got a two-week wait to see if this egg sticks. They give you a pregnancy test and tell you exactly what day to take it on. It's the worst two weeks of your life, you're constantly wanting to take a pregnancy test and constantly scrutinising every twinge and symptom. Hurry up!

Dun dun dun… test day. The accumulation of four months of hard work mentally, physically and usually financially (this round was NHS funded) comes down to this three-minute, and hopeful two pink lines test… actually shitting myself. I couldn't sleep so I got up at 5 am and I go ahead and do it whilst shaking (not too much, don't want pee on me). This is it, the rest of our life can begin now, we can have our own little family we've dreamt of for so long. I go back to the bathroom and what the fuck: it's negative. It can't be, we put so much effort into this — no, no, no! My husband goes back to the bathroom to check it again… oh here come the waterworks.

Someone swallow me up and drown me with alcohol. I'm shaking, puking and the world is falling out my arse — not a good look but that's what stress does to you ladies and gentlemen.

The next few weeks I was graced with all the drugs coming out and a delightfully heavy period — thanks for adding that extra shit storm! It's ok, it's ok I've still got two eggs in the freezer- phew. The day after my failure, I don't give myself time to think or grieve, I want to know when I can do my next round! The clinic advise that I need to wait until my next period before I can start: excellent, that's what I'll do. I'm not stopping for anything; I want this family so badly.

We go in to discuss things with the clinic and they're happy for us to have our last two eggs put back at the same time if we want, even though it increases the risk of having twins. Fuck it, I've been waiting for this, if I can have twins then this is a winner. Again, no counselling, so I just sail through and push on with the next round. I can't remember much of this one because it was a long time ago and it's all a bit of a blur, though I think I had to do most of what I did before (with the injections) I didn't have to have that last injection because I wasn't going into surgery as we already have the fertilised eggs. The injections this time just had to take over my cycle and get my womb lining ready to accept the little frozen buggers.

The clinic did warn us that our eggs could die during the unfreezing process so that means we could do all these drugs and the clinic could call us on the morning of the procedure to say our eggs had died. This IVF is just an awful horrible waiting game, full of anxiety and waiting around. Can you see how unbelievably frustrating and emotional this process is now? Can you see why I get so upset when I hear a pregnancy announcement when I'm trying so bloody hard just to get just that far?!!

It's also extremely draining on your relationship — forget normal sex, lust and fun times during this process. All that shit goes right out the window and replaced with emotional turmoil and stress. It's a wonder anyone who fails at IVF stays together!

Well, me eggs luckily didn't die so I had the procedure and again, I believe we had a coffee and cake instead of a slap-up English grill. The dreaded two weeks wait again… ah, fucking hell, I've got butterflies already.

Test day… dun dun dun. Yep, you guessed it: 'not pregnant.' My world collapsed again; I'm sad and angry all in one I'm shaking, puking and shitting again. I hate this bloody IVF process and I hate life. Why can't I just be happy? Where is my luck in this world?

When I've calmed down as much as I can, I call the clinic and tell them the results. They said they were sorry and said if we wanted to make a follow-up appointment to discuss things we could. How in the hell is that gonna help? There were no other calls and I didn't want to go back to that place again; they'd washed their hands of me.

The Ugly Chrysalis

Sometimes I just want someone to hug me and say, "I know it's hard. You're going to be okay. Here's some chocolate and £5 million."

Chapter 6
Counselling with some booze

It was at this stage in my life that booze took on a new form of its own. Two failed IVFs, years of trying to conceive and no funds to afford to go private at that point (pay for it ourselves). Well, that's it, ladies and gentlemen, this is my life. What the hell do I do now? Everything I have ever dreamed of, hold on — most people dream of — has just fallen in front of me and a little devil appeared on my shoulder and said, "No, you can't have that life so ha-ha. No living legacy or happy family for you my dear." Well, I say, "Cheers for that, you can fuck off now!" Now, I need to get down the pub.

Cue the pub, which became my best friend almost every evening. I didn't think I had a problem back then; I didn't even contemplate what I was doing. All I knew was that I was stuck with this situation that I really didn't want to be in, or know how to deal with. Nothing prepares you for this unknown existence. I mean there aren't any books or guidance from the clinic, schools or parents or anyone to tell you what to do with your life if you can't have, what basically almost the entire world can have: kids! I didn't know there was such a life to contemplate, why would I have ever considered this? No one else I know has, it just isn't something that's talked about in society and you just don't think about that when your entire life is aimed towards meeting 'the one,' buying a house, getting married and having a family; it's what most girls dream about.

There are the ladies and men out there that, granted, don't want a family and they get on with their life and are very happy. I have great respect for them, but there is a difference: their decision was a conscious one that they've made and they're happy with that decision. They have direction in their life and know what they want. My predicament was not a decision I made; it was a decision given to me that I didn't want, so of course, I'm going to resist accepting it and try to create a new life.

So, to contemplate this dilemma, I decided that I needed to drown out the noise in my head and not think about it. If I can't have kids then what's the next best thing in my life? Drinking and going out whenever you like, because you don't have kids; you tell yourself that this is what your life will be, it's the best thing for me. In my head I was thinking, "Yeah, I mean look at all my friends with their ruddy perfect families. Well, they're obviously not as happy as we are because we're still living the dream of going out when we like with no ties." Well, it didn't work out quite like that with a happy drunk ending; it's sooo not the case because the friends with a family are happy, it's what they wanted.

In the months after the failed IVFs, I got angrier and angrier. If I didn't go to the pub, I would throw a full-on fit. My poor husband had to put up with whatever was happening and go with the flow. He always said to me he would be happy either way to have kids or not, so long as I'm happy. I mean, that is a truly lovely husband right there, but me being me took that as, well, he obviously doesn't care about the failed IVF and it doesn't mean that much to him. This stayed in my head for a long time and I didn't communicate much with him or even acknowledge that he might be suffering as well. Yes, I was a bad wife in that respect, but I was so consumed with the fact that I was useless because I couldn't give us the life we longed for. I couldn't put anyone else's feelings above my own. Just a heads up: that doesn't work in the relationship world, it really does make you not like one another. We didn't talk about it; I didn't see the point and that wasn't a good thing to do.

The lazy spa (hot-tub) became a whole new pub all on its own; we would fill weekends and even some evenings inviting whoever would come round to our house to party and get utterly shitfaced in our tub. We positioned it just outside our garage in the back garden near the beer fridge — bloody perfect, we don't have to go anywhere now and I can be a dribbling mess in my own house behind closed doors where no one can see or judge me.

There were two pubs we frequented within walking distance and there were a lot of evenings down both of them (from what I remember), where we would start all happy and okay together then as the evening went on, we would start to crack and have arguments. We couldn't be bothered to cook and ate a lot of takeaways late at night, after we'd consumed most of the bar, of course. In fact, we even got to know the barman at one of the pubs — that defo meant we were there far too often. I went into a drinking depressive state for about six months.

About the end of November, I was sitting in my living room writing out Christmas cards - yes, I'm one of them mad people who buys and writes out Christmas cards and get the tree up as early as it's acceptable because I love Christmas even though I can't share it with my own little family. Millie Moo and Poppy were sat in their beds when all of a sudden, Millie Moo started panting and crying in pain. I rushed over and took her out of the bed. She was all stiff and couldn't walk. I began to realise she had a problem with her back. Simon was out at the time, but I immediately called him and he rushed home.

We'd both watched a TV program on Channel 4 called Fitzpatrick Referral's. Noel Fitzpatrick (nicknamed the Bionic Vet or Super Vet) is an amazing chap who's pioneered surgery for all animals that no other vet has done. He has a private referral centre in Eashing for surgery and recovery and a referral centre in Guildford which is for the treatment of cancer.

I had heard of Intervertebral Disc Disease (IVDD) which is what I suspected Millie Moo had but I didn't know much about it. I did, however, know it's vital to get your dog looked at as quickly as possible if you suspect they may be having an IVDD episode to determine what the best course of action should be. IVDD is, in laymen's terms, the jelly in between your discs on your back. Well, in dogs it explodes upward and puts pressure on the spinal cord; the longer it's left like that, the bigger the chance of paralysis. If a dog has IVDD, it's most likely been born with it and sadly it occurs in dogs with long backs. So, not allowing them to jump on and off furniture or up and down the stairs when they're younger can prevent this from occurring, but sadly if it's going to happen there is nothing you can do to stop it. I believe there is now a test they can carry out on a puppy to see if it has IVDD but this wasn't a thing when I got mine.

So, we both agreed that we would get Millie Moo into Fitzpatrick Referrals. We called them and explained the situation; they agreed we should come down straightaway but to call our vet and get them to send over her records en route. When we got there, we were booked in and sat in the waiting area for a short period of time, before seeing one of Noel's team. When we were called in, the lady examined Millie Moo and immediately suspected IVDD but Millie Moo would need to be left with them that day to carry out an MRI. After which, they would call to determine the next steps and possible surgery that day.

We left Mille Moo in their capable hands; our hearts were beating out of our chests the whole way home. We held on to Poppy as she was distressed from the panicking ordeal and didn't understand why Millie Moo wasn't with us when we left. An agonising hour later, Fitzpatrick's called to say that Millie Moo had stage five IVDD and would require surgery on her back to have any sort of fighting chance at walking again. We couldn't believe it, but we gave the go-ahead as we felt she had a good chance of recovering as she was only young; they did the operation that day.

Fitzpatrick called us again later that evening to say that Millie Moo's operation had gone well and she was now recovering in the intensive care unit. She will remain there and be monitored over the next few days and they will work with her doing physiotherapy and hydrotherapy to stimulate her spinal nerve to get her to walk and go to the toilet again.

We were both having a really hard time dealing with the loss of our IVF transfers that year and I was struggling with my drinking, so this just topped things off and made us even more unhappy than we already were! We had to try and be strong for Millie Moo and Poppy. I'd signed up for a Santa fun run at work to raise funds for a local hospice. I felt sad and worried about Millie Moo the entire time because we all wanted her back for Christmas. Millie Moo was supposed to do the fun run with us.

Dear Lucy, Poppy and Millie

On behalf of Phyllis Tuckwell Hospice Care, I wanted to write to tha Rudolph Fun Run 2016 at the Queens Avenue Playing Fields, Aldershot and for raising a fantastic £204.70 in sponsorship.

2016 saw us returning to Aldershot, Hindhead and Godalming for another successful year. It was wonderful to see over 650 participants taking part in the runs and raising money for Phyllis Tuckwell.

Please do pass on our thanks and appreciation to all your family friends and colleagues who have sponsored you and thank you to you for all your fundraising efforts. We are very excited to say the three events combined have already raised over £18,000 which is a

You will be aware that al patients and their familie our total costs, we have our full range of service part in the Santa & Ru care to the 250 patients every day. We would Tuckwell Hospice Care us for many more years

We couldn't let the team down, so me and Poppy did our run and raised £204.70.

Poppy and I claimed our badge of honour without Millie Moo.

That next week we got daily updates; the nurses looking after Millie Moo said she was walking and going to the toilet and they were getting her strength up. She was going to hydrotherapy and physiotherapy every day still and was a little character — they even put a swimming costume on

Moo (ha-ha). They agreed we could come in at the weekend to collect Millie Moo. I've got a video of it so I can't share the utter excitement from both parties but believe me, we had a massive cuddle and a cry in the clinic at the joy of seeing her again; she's our little girl.

We didn't know what to expect with Millie Moo's mobility so we left Poppy at home with Simon's mum whilst we collected Millie Moo. It had been almost three weeks since we'd seen her. We made the decision not to visit her whilst she was recovering so as not to confuse and upset her. It was so, so very hard but we were glad the day was here to collect our baby in time for Christmas.

The vet sat and talked to us in her room before we left and explained that sadly, all the way down her spine, she has IVDD, so we will need to be extra careful with her from now on. No jumping on and off anything or going up or down any stairs. We immediately put up baby gates top and bottom of the stairs and set about teaching them both not to jump on and off anything anymore. Knowing what I know now, I wish I'd never allowed that to happen.

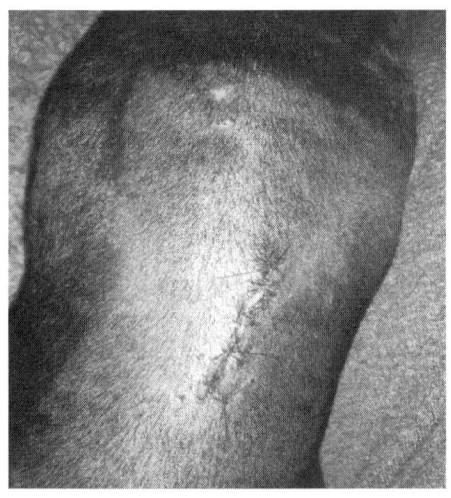

This is Millie Moo's scar on her back — ouch!

When we picked Millie Moo up, we paid the enormous £5,500 bill ($6,861). Oh, thank god for insurance! The drive home was scary; Millie Moo was disoriented and crying so we had to be as careful as we could. I held her in the back whilst Simon drove.

My good friend Debbie who owns large, beautiful Alsatian dogs had a spare extra-large crate which she let us borrow whilst Millie Moo was recovering. I can't tell you how grateful I was to have this.

I mean this thing is big! We all got in it and I comforted Mille Moo so she didn't feel left out or distressed.

Poppy was confused and didn't understand what was wrong with Millie Moo; we let her gently sniff Moo's wound. She smelt like a hospital and none of us liked it much but it would take time to get her back to smelling like us again.

Millie Moo took about three months to get back her strength. We had to take her to the physiotherapy and hydrotherapy at Fitzpatrick every week and continue doing physiotherapy as much as we could at home. This cost us an extra £1,500 ($1,871) out of our own money but it's for Millie Moo, so we didn't care. We both had separate weeks off work. My mum and Simon's mum helped out with coming over during the following weeks and caring for Millie Moo whilst we went back to work. We all pitched in to get Millie Moo better and we would have been lost without the help.

Sadly, things got so bad between Simon and I in the meantime, with all the stress, we were almost hitting the divorce stage and everything was getting on top of us. Simon moved out to his parents for a break after Millie Moo was getting better as we really couldn't take the arguing anymore. I hated my life and I wanted it all to end, there was no happiness just always it seemed, very unlucky.

When I got back to work after caring for Millie Moo and Simon was moved out, I all of a sudden just fell to the floor in the office, crying my eyes out and hyperventilating. Bearing in mind I'd not spoken to any family, work colleagues or friends about any of my 'behind-the-scenes-relationship,'
because why would you? I just carried on as normal in front of them; I couldn't let them see me as a weak person who couldn't get on with my life. I don't like to burden people with my problems... which is possibly a downfall for me. A lady who worked with me took me into her office, sat

me down and told me her story. She'd never spoken about it before and you'd never know that she'd gone through the same process (that's how I wanted to come across), she told me I needed to go back to the clinic and get counselling.

Before I could do the counselling, Simon moved back in. We had a heart to heart; we knew this wasn't going to be an easy ride for either of us so I decided I wanted a quick break away from it all and went away for a weekend with my mum to Poland. Whilst there we visited Auschwitz. What a truly amazing place to visit, it definitely puts your own sadness into perspective that's for sure!

As you can see, I had a good time but I know that sadly, I drank far too much on that break. I was hiding and running away from things again, but you can't tell, can you?

When I got back, it was on to counselling. Oh Jesus, I've got to walk up these stairs at that very same IVF clinic and sit in the same room where all the couples trying for an IVF baby are — fuck I want to throw up! I did it and got to the counselling sessions. After seven or so sessions I did start to feel better, I knew this was a long road but Simon had moved back and we were getting on with life as best we could. If someone had told me that I should have gone to counselling during and after the IVF, that would have been most helpful! For God's sake — trying to navigate this ruddy process is a nightmare.

Counselling went through a lot of emotions, as you can imagine. To get to the crux of why I was hurting it came down to a number of things:

- I was sad that my dad had another family and is now a step-grandad which for me really hurt as this was all happening while we were trying for a baby and pursuing the IVF. I'm sad that I'll never be able to provide that. It's not his fault whatsoever; it's just the way I feel and you cannot help how you feel about things.
- Being told things like, "You can be the best Auntie," or "It's not the end of the world," or "Other people have worse problems." All these words affected me. It made me feel like my childlessness was discounted and just something I should just 'get over' and 'be happy with what I've got.' It's hard to

explain to people that it's a lifelong process that will keep coming up my entire life and it's just not that easy. I always think: would these people actually say these things to someone who'd physically lost a baby? No, they bloody wouldn't but it's what's happened to me. I've lost a life and I'm grieving an entire lost life, so I should be treated with the same respect.

- The counselling highlighted that I feel I can't have a strong bond with my own mum over having a baby and spend time with her and a grandchild.
- I was also dealing with the trauma of the surgeries with both dogs.
- Lastly, my relationship with my sister had completely broken down. I felt like she doesn't want

to be there for me and that she had replaced me with her best friend.

Listen, no one has a perfect family; everyone has their problems, but these are my shitty problems in my head that for some reason make me want to drink and hide away from everyone. I needed to understand why I felt like I did so I could get out of my funk. Counselling should be on anyone's list who has had trauma — well, that would be the whole world then! Seriously, it helps you look at things from a different perspective and it's good to talk to someone outside of 'your people!'

The counsellor suggested a few things that helped:

- One thing was to write a letter to my 'child / children' apologising for not being able to meet him/her and writing everything you're going to miss in his / her life and to say goodbye. She suggested I either keep the letter or burn it as a way of release.

- The next thing was to either bury or burn my IVF papers or anything that related to it as this can be a powerful way of releasing any anger towards the process. Well, I love a BBQ, so we lit the BBQ one evening and burnt every single page one by one, and it felt good.
- I was holding on to some of my nan's ashes (Betty) and the counsellor suggested I release them in a happy place. So we went down to Worthing (a seaside town for my American friends) my nan loved this place,

and we released the tiny bit I had into the sea to say goodbye.

All these things were extremely powerful and overwhelming at the time but slowly, I began to feel a bit better. I'm aware that grief takes a long time and I believe, even though I had counselling and it was helpful, it didn't stop me walking about like a zombie, watching everyone else enjoy their life for a good six months, I felt completely numb — like the life had been drained out of me.

We went on holiday to Rome in May 2017 to try and cheer ourselves up but again, finding the nearest bar serving alcohol was a top priority — obviously!

As you can see, I very much enjoyed a pint in an ice-cold glass in Rome.

Don't get me wrong, we did go sight-seeing before we drank the beer so it wasn't a total waste. We didn't have any arguments either which was a winner, but I could feel we were very far apart. I hadn't dealt with all the demons in my head about not being able to have children and the truth is, I didn't know how to fight them, I only had a limited amount of counselling with the clinic and after all that IVF expenditure I didn't' think it would be necessary to pay out for anymore. I felt like a holiday would be more worth it at the time.

Simon was quiet and we didn't talk about it much either; it was as if the IVF hadn't happened and so we shouldn't talk about it. Neither of us knew what to say to one another. Simon managed to not get as drunk as me, like I said he could take it or leave it; he's one of those people who just quietly gets on with things and doesn't make a fuss. Well I wanted to make a fuss and I wanted to talk about it all but for some reason I just couldn't. Looking back, I now realise we were at different stages and grieving differently.

The day we got back from Rome was a disaster, we went back to pick up Poppy and Millie Moo. During the evening, sadly, Poppy went down crying in pain. We knew it was IVDD from what we'd been through with Millie Moo.

Poppy had never been covered on her insurance for anything to do with her back since she was rushed into the vet as a puppy. On her notes, it had said minor back pain but nothing had ever come of it and annoyingly, the insurance company had refused to cover her back from then on. This meant we would be paying out ourselves privately and having just come back from an expensive trip to Rome we were feeling broke... really, right now? This can't be happening; we tried to do something nice and then it turned into months of stress! It wasn't beloved Poppy's fault; bless her, we would do anything for our pups.

My stepsister worked in a referral clinic at the time and the owner had five dachshunds so he was well aware of

IVDD. We booked Poppy in that day for an MRI after seeing the vet in a consultation.

Poppy wasn't in as much pain as Millie Moo was, she just couldn't stand on her back legs and was shaking. We left her with the vet to carry out the operation. This time it only cost £3,000 ($3,741) but it was out of our own money and that was a stinger but we didn't care; we stuck it on a credit card. Poppy was worth every penny and I would pay every time for my dogs because you'd do the same for any family member.

We got sent a picture of Pops in recovery and we were allowed to collect her a week after her operation. Aww bless her, she looked so cute.

We set up the crate just like we had done for Millie Moo and let her rest and recover.

Poppy didn't need any help with physiotherapy or hydrotherapy, she was up and walking the next week with no misfunction in her legs. It was so good to see her back to normal and a relief for all of us.

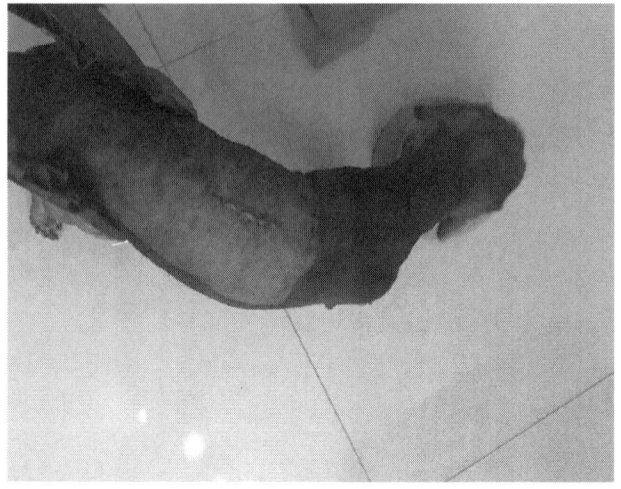

Over the next few years, I didn't really function very well. I was just an angry upset person and no one understood my pain so hiding away became the go-to thing again.

I stopped seeing my friends, mainly because they had babies and for some reason, the pregnant part and baby part, even to this day, still hurts my heart. My dad's family were starting to have children and this became another impossible set of emotions to deal with because no one understood me. I suspect to this day most people thought I was being selfish and horrible but no one took the time to understand me so I hid away because as soon as you start talking about your struggles, no one gets it. It was just easier to stay away from everyone and protect my feelings.

To this day, I still have to turn over the TV if there are any pregnant people or babies on there. Even in real life, I avoid putting myself in a situation where there might be babies or pregnant people; it's a way of protecting my heart so I don't have a meltdown and everyone stare at me. I could, in time, be okay with these situations, like I'm okay now with toddlers but that took a lot of years just to be okay with, and to me, that's okay. It's an achievement on my part for what I've been through. I have to be kind to myself and not worry about what others think too much.

No one will completely understand what it's like to not be able to conceive unless it's happening to them. However, if you ask people with children if they would swap places, I guarantee you they wouldn't for one minute because that's the life they wanted and they love their kids. Oh, actually, they might give you some smart arse answer like "I'd love to swap it must be great not having kids, you can do what you want all the time,"… yes I'm sure that's the case for people who CHOOSE to live that life and guess what, you had that option yourself. Your own parents are the same, they try to say something comforting like "I'm sure it will happen," or "It's not the end of the world,"- wow really? Not the end of the world?! I really want to say, "So what on earth would you have done in my situation back in your day? Do you really think it's that easy to just 'move on?" Come on now, this is a lifetime adjustment. This wasn't a choice! I'm lost, confused and upset. I'm not bloody happy, content and have a path in life, im lost.

All I ever want to hear is "I'm here for you" and for people to be kind and sympathetic to my situation and not force me or put me in a room full of kids or people with kids — you're seriously hurting me when you do this. How can I join in?

Send me a separate text telling me about a pregnancy announcement and ask if I'm okay. I will 100% have a meltdown, that's standard. I'm happy for you but it brings back a tsunami of sadness because of my own situation so don't be offended when I don't contact you because I'm dealing with an overwhelming state of mind just be as kind as you would be to someone who has lost a close family member because that's all we want`. Sadly no one does this, they avoid telling the childless person and let them find out via the grape vine but then wonder why the childless person is the way she is towards them.

We've got to find a new way of living and a new life. That shit takes a monumental amount of grieving, effort and time to do, a whole lifetime, in fact.

Most people just assume because you can't have a baby you can just get on with life; they don't realise that it's a grieving process. I'm grieving for a life I can no longer have. Just because you can't physically see the loss of a human being doesn't mean you can simply move on. Just stop for one minute and think about how you would cope. You have to cope because there's no other way; it's just a very, very long tough way.

Talk to me, ask me how I am, ask me about how I cope and really listen to me with understanding; don't chime in with witty answers or stupid suggestions like 'relax and it will happen.' I've visited enough bloody doctors who've told me my predicament so don't downgrade my problem!

Offer to come to counselling with me, read online about others in the same situation; get knowledgeable so you can understand me on some level. Don't be afraid to ask me things. If you ask questions it shows you're taking an interest and trying to understand my situation. Don't leave me out, take special time to be with me because I matter as well and I need your support more than most.

Just realise it takes a toll on your mental, physical and financial health. So yeah, all that money you were intending on spending on the non-existent 'grandkids' or 'niece/nephew' I don't have, please go ahead and spend it on me; I need a nice book or some retail therapy money or that lunch out or a holiday. Make me feel like not being able to have kids means I can be spoilt as well... It's not too much to ask for, is it? Plus Christmas is not just for bloody kids! It's for me as well!

Ok that's enough sadness for one chapter, you get the picture by now — don't let me sink into the background and drink myself to death, just bloody be there for me! In fact, be there for my lifetime, like you would if I had cancer or lost someone! It's not that ruddy difficult, people.

Oh, and might I add I lost my best friend (Betty) who was my dad's mum right when I was just about to start my first lot of IVF, so that also didn't help with my mental state. Then I lost my other nan, mum's mum (Gladys) just after we finished our frozen round; sadly I wasn't that close to her but I know my mum was extremely sad and that also hurt me to see. So, I conclude that this year has been full of lots of loss and sadness.

Dear life, is there a break yet? No, don't be silly I need to chuck some more shit at you first! (evil laugh).

Here is the lovely Betty at my wedding. She was always there; she was my rock but I didn't/don't have that friend to fall back on anymore. I stood proudly at her funeral and read a beautiful poem for her; it's up there with one of my hardest things I've done in my life so far.

And breathe... let's sing the happy song — one, two, three...

Chapter 7
A Punch up in The Uterus

Simon and I figured we'd been through a heck of a ride so why can't we treat ourselves?

Simon wanted a fast BMW, so cue the entrance of Boyce in August 2017 who is now mine because Simon's been given a vehicle through his work: winner. I would like a trip of a lifetime to Canada please.

I wanted to go on the Rocky Mountaineer, I knew it would cost a bomb but who cares? We deserved it. I sat for hours searching the hotels and which places to visit. We decided to go in September the following year; we told our family and I asked my mum to look after the sausages — perfect. We put our deposit down for our two-week holiday for September 2018... woohoo!

My sister got engaged a month after we had booked our holiday; we all had a great time at the party – yes lots of alcohol. We have a family tradition that someone gets the ugly wooden chicken. It does the rounds around the family; it stayed with Dad after Mum and Dad split up and it was so ugly no one wanted it, so Dad decided one Christmas that it would make a great present to get rid of it — good one!

It continued its rounds over the years and my dad and his wife even took it to New York and took a picture of it on a bridge. They told us they'd left it there... ha-ha, well I got this delightful wooden chicken as an extra wedding present a few years later… bloody liars. I'd decided to keep it for many years until my sister got engaged — bam, here you go woman. It was a funny moment, she loved and hated it. So now everyone dreads opening presents on 'special' occasions.

Sadly, my sister and I have had a rocky relationship over the years. I won't go into details. You can't get on with everyone all of the time, I guess, and everyone has spats with their siblings from time to time.

After all the rubbish that had gone on in our life beforehand, my complete change of character came when my sister announced her wedding date would be in September 2018 which was the same time as my amazing two week holiday… you are fucking kidding me, right? Everyone knows about our holiday, texts were even sent out asking about everyone's holidays for the next year so schedules didn't clash.

Now bear in mind that I had to book the time off work and, my husband had to book someone to cover for him; he runs his own business and it's near on impossible for him to get time off. So, our plans were in full swing for this holiday before the wedding date was decided.

Sadly, we had to change our plans and all I could think was, our plans for our entire life have continually changed and the one stable happy thing we had booked to bring some happiness into our life was over before it began. We were both truly upset and angry that we couldn't seem to catch a break. It felt like no one was listening to us.

I got phone call after phone call from everyone, trying to get me to go to the wedding, saying that it's important and that my holiday could wait. That was it; I'd had enough of everything. The wedding date wasn't going to change so another blow to our already shit life; we had to cancel our holiday because we had no one to look after the dogs and we lost our deposit – we were totally gutted at this stage. My personality had completely changed; I was one angry motherfucker.

We proceeded to book a caravan holiday (a slight downgrade) for the week of the wedding and we were going no matter what! We booked with friends and the dogs could come with us.

In the meantime, the forces that be didn't want to let us have any good luck or whatever you want to call it and gave us another shit storm. This time it was Millie Moo's turn to go down with IVDD again in September

2017 which was just after Poppy had returned to normal in May!

Honestly, my life felt like an episode of EastEnders! (For those of you who don't know what that is, it's a UK soap on TV that airs every week following the stories of local residents as they go through life — it's full of drama!) Drama and trauma are two words that come up a lot in my life.

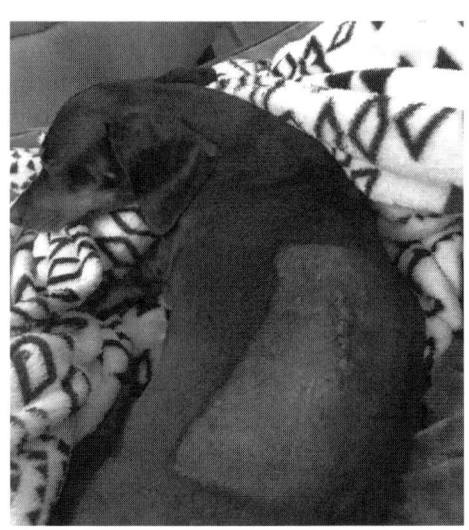

Sadly, poor Millie Moo struggled to return to normal after her second operation and struggled to walk. Can you see her old scar and her new one from the operation in this picture? Poor little mite.

As soon as she was able to, after lots of rest, recuperation and again, help from the mums, we booked Millie Moo into a local rehab centre for physiotherapy and hydrotherapy. It was a lot closer to home which made it easier. Millie Moo on the treadmill… go Mille Moo!

Again, we spent a lot of time getting her back to as normal as possible. Sadly, she wasn't going to be able to use one of her back legs very well but it's okay because Moo got her five minutes of TV fame when hoodad was caught giving her a kiss on the head in the Fitzpatrick Referral's waiting room. Ha-ha brilliant.

And here he is smouching Millie Moo.

Ok, so by now you all realise I'm a raging alcoholic — well it feels like it even if I don't portray myself that way — I'm a functioning one.

I'm feeling 'okay-ish' most days, just getting through each day as it comes really, not really knowing what is going to happen and still don't know what my life is really about: a zombie state still. Still going down the pub most days, I think I would be very rich if I added up how much we spent on booze — how annoying!

I did decide that it would be a good idea (god knows why) to have a neighbour's party to cheer us up, it was in autumn so it wasn't an outdoor BBQ. It was just a chilled evening in, ha-ha. We got a lot of booze and food; in fact, I think we spent about £150 on just that night. I got a table full of posh nibbles to soak up the booze. We got ten bottles of red and ten bottles of white, plus ten bottles of Prosecco, three boxes of different beers and a few gins and vodkas with a selection of mixers; we don't like to disappoint our guests, you see. Well, they came over about 6ish (from what I remember) and most had already eaten, so no one really ate the food but we did put a dent in the alcohol.

I'm not sure why my brain didn't think about this… hold on a minute there are only about ten people coming, you definitely don't need that much alcohol. At least two of them don't really drink much and people usually bring a bottle or two of their own and they live like two seconds away so I'm pretty sure they all have a supply of alcohol in their own house if you run out! I can only conclude that my brain thought, hold on we'd better make sure we don't run out of alcohol for you to drink on the night, so get extra for yourself!

Well most of them got very drunk. Obviously I got the drunkest because I went upstairs to the toilet then decided a quick kip was in order, only to wake up the next morning still in my clothes sprawled out on the bed. Oh, what a hangover! Can I just say that prosecco is the worst for a bad head! All I could think was, I hope I didn't do or say anything embarrassing! Apparently, I didn't because they all spoke to me in the following days — phew.

Here is a little snippet of the kitchen from the night before.

I've got an idea! Let's not do that one again. Ok, deal!

So, we decided that we'd had enough of Farnborough. Simon's work was moving and we have to go where his job was so we scoped out some houses in a few lovely villages and eventually went to see this dream house in a country village. The only criteria on our list was that it needed to be within walking distance of a local pub… tick. We walked around it once, yes just once, got in our car got halfway down the road pulled over and both said we want that house let's put in an offer. Woo hoo, offer accepted: £495,000 ($621,691) boom, pop in the local for a swift one. I worked for solicitors so had my work do my conveyancing which didn't amount to much of a discount, you'd think the staff would get it free wouldn't you as a little perk? Yeah right, same as every job I guess!

So, we just got on with drinking continually, life was a bit stagnant waiting for this move, with the chain being complicated it took months so that didn't help the bottle count. We booked a weekend away to New York to cheer ourselves up in February 2018 and obviously this was filled with booze and fun together, which we needed!

No one told me that bloody ghostbusters were in New York town, I'm so glad I found them; I always knew there were ghosts about haha. Obviously, a standard cosmopolitan cocktail or ten were obligatory in New York as well.

In the meantime, what started to get worse was my stomach pain. I needed the toilet an awful lot. I mean, I know I drink a lot and I had just put it down to that over the years, but it was getting worse. The pain and symptoms I had I just couldn't ignore anymore. So, I trotted along to the doc and listed all my symptoms, she immediately said it sounds like you've got endometriosis. I'm sorry an endo what-ness?

Then she explained that bits of tissue that line your uterus grows on other pelvic organs like your ovaries or tubes. Ewwww, that sounds gross and cancer-y, like a growth taking over my innards. Suddenly I get an image of that scene out of alien where it pops through the stomach with an alien head…ha-ha. Concentrate woman, this is serious she's now said she's sending you for a laparoscopy. I'm sorry a lap what copy? Ohh, it's keyhole surgery… WHAT?! I've never been cut into, in my life; anything I've had done when I've been under has been through holes I already own. Oh, Jesus I'm gonna look like Frankenstein. Ok, ok calm down.

So, it's surgery to remove as much of the endo as possible, the snag is… der

der der... there is no cure! Oh, brills so I do this ruddy surgery for nothing. She explains that unfortunately, it does affect fertility and it will grow back but it usually takes about five years before you need any more surgery. Ok well, that's cool that's quite a long time.

So, it's scheduled for the end of June 2018, and in the meantime, I Google the shit out of endo and the operation to find out what I can, it mentions, depending on the severity of the endo and what they remove will dictate your recovery time, anything up to eight weeks. Well, work is going to love that one! I tell work about all this but conclude that I will probably be off about two weeks; I mean it can't be that bad inside.

I decided that in order to be in the best body shape for the operation, I need to not drink. I was truly terrified of having surgery — having never had any before it scared me so I thought giving up alcohol before surgery would give me the best fighting chance at getting better quickly. Time to give up the booze — I actually managed to do this six weeks before my surgery... bloody hell I can do this (but I really want a glass of wine).

Surgery day: oh Christ, complete waterworks and breakdown being wheeled into surgery, hyperventilating, panicking, ahhhh! The nice nurses calm me down and give me some of that wonderful drug that you count to one, two, three gone. Wakey, wakey "doc, doc I really, really need a wee." "It's ok Lucy you don't need a wee, you've just come round from surgery and are confused." Well, this morphine is a winner. Bear in mind this is supposed to be day surgery, I can't do anything by halves so I have to stay in overnight because I've got low blood pressure, not what I had planned on this evening I must say. I wanted bloody chocolate cake!

The surgeon comes round to see me a few hours later and explained I had stage four endo (the most severe) all over me ovaries plus deep endo pushing on my bladder and a few polyps — well who would have thought I'd have that much going on in there, what a party! He also said he was signing me off work for four weeks total rest. Oh, bloody hell, work isn't gonna be happy about that... and they weren't overly happy because they only paid me for two weeks, not four, and didn't tell me until I found out on payday that month — cheers for that, could have given me the heads up I might have tried to come in or do something to get paid I do have a mortgage for Pete's sake... why is this a saying, who is Pete anyway?

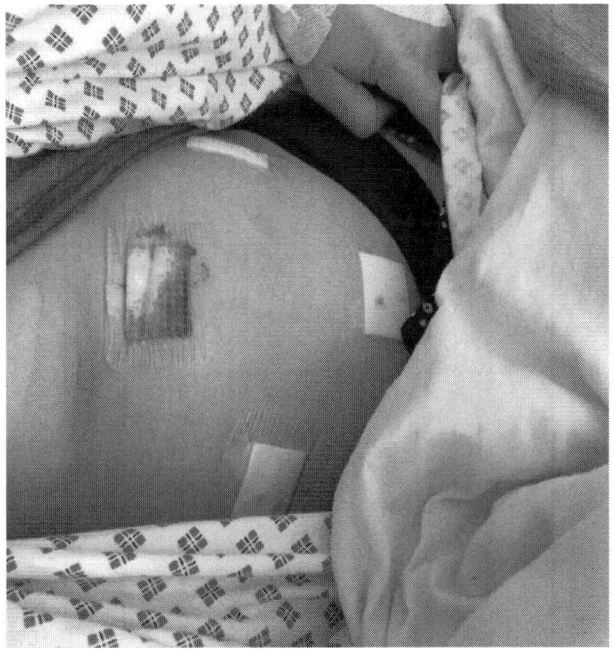

Anyway, so here it is: the huge bruised belly. Might I add that I had rather a lovely flat-ish stomach before surgery? Luckily my husband left me with Netflix on a working laptop to indulge in, but after all the drama, I passed out anyway.

I wasn't allowed out until mid-afternoon the next day, so frustrating — bloody blood pressure. Probably all that alcohol I had poured down my neck over the years making me blood flow run slow — I'm joking, I don't think so!

So most of July 2018 was fabulous because the weather was amazing and I could sit out in me garden with the sausages, plus Farnborough Air Show was due to commence so there were a lot of planes and jets flying over doing stunts which I never got bored of and I had a few visitors over.

After the endo operation, the Surgeon said that the next six months would be a good time to try and conceive naturally before going down any IVF route again. So, we did and I can tell you that one month (well actually every month for seven bloody years) I was thinking this might be it, I might be pregnant. Then the dreaded period comes and you get sad. It's a full-time job having all these emotions every single month of your life for your child-bearing years and a week of your month wanting to hide away and scream at the world.

This particular month, I hadn't done any tests but I had the worst period of my entire life. Sorry, this is gross people; we were out food shopping but I had to rush home because I could feel things coming out of me. When we got home, I ran into the shower and stood under the hot water for three minutes whilst what looked like my entire womb fall out of me and the worst pain I've ever felt. It calmed down after a few hours and I made an appointment with the doctor the next day. The doctor couldn't confirm it was a miscarriage because I hadn't done a pregnancy test but he confirmed it sounded like one. He just told me to rest up and I will be fine next month. Ohh ok, will do Doc.

So, end of July 2018, well what do you know, completion is due on the 30th and the day before completion I go back to work! I have to politely ask if I can take a few days off to move… awkward, after just having a month off recovering from surgery but fuck it I need to move so it's tough, sack me if you wish. Hold on don't, I need to afford this beast of a house.

We moved into our beautiful four-bed, three-bathroom gated driveway with enough room to fit nine cars on house... this is when we knew we'd made it in life. Hold on though, don't just assume because I have a lovely house and I portray a lovely life to you on social media or face to face, that I actually have a lovely life. I'm usually hiding a whirlwind of shit inside and I am desperately trying not to cry the entire time — just know that and don't judge me.

I mean we've added on an extra bedroom and two extra bathrooms in the hopes of filling these with chubby little Lucy and Simon's one day... to be honest, this house is beautiful but what is the point in a lovely family house that's empty- yep fuck all point at all just a shit load more to clean, we may as well live in a shed. The empty bedrooms are a constant reminder of the children we haven't got. It's okay though because we got a brand new American style flashy fridge to go in the kitchen- fill her up with booze.

This village is very community-spirited, it's peaceful and it's a wonderful place to bring up children. The only snag is we are about an hour's drive from friends and family and don't have children... bummer. Needs must, you have to go with the flow and go where the money is at the end of the day. I'm sure we will make new friends (cough) *drinking buddies,* down the local.

In the meantime, my fat belly healed quite a lot but not completely cause I'm still fat! What the f did that doc do because it certainly wasn't a bit of lypo! Wanna see...?

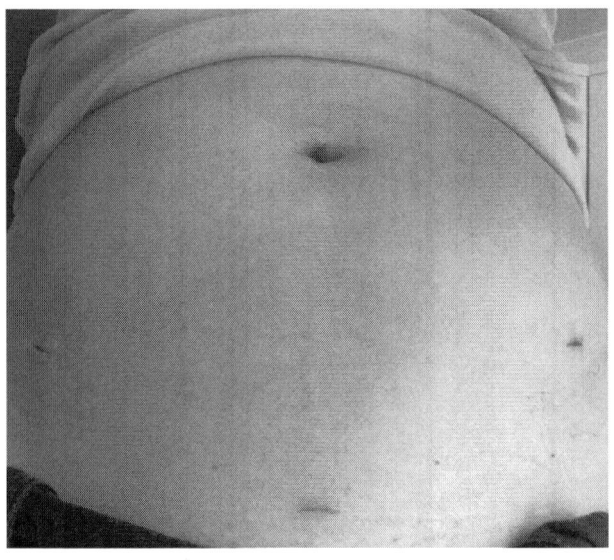

I mean the scars have now healed to a point where you can't even see where they were which is great... I've still got a slight muffin top though. (A sad face is happening now, whilst belly pinching).

Everyone was really happy for us with our move but my mum was upset that it was a long way from her as she can't come over to see us anymore, and she doesn't want to drive that far as it gives her anxiety driving on a motorway. I understood, but it really upset me. I've just had to accept there isn't anything I can do about it. I live in hope that someday she will turn up at mine having driven over herself and I'd be so proud of her.

September 2018 came and went and yes, we didn't go to the wedding and we had an okay time on our substitute caravan holiday to Poole with our friends and the dogs.

Over the months after my sister's wedding, I felt awful and extremely sad because we'd lost each other. All I've ever really wanted was a sister and a friend. Someone to confide in, someone to keep an eye on me, someone to have coffee and cake with, but sadly it just has never been that way with us and I expected too much. I was full of anxiety over everything that had happened in the last year but for me, I knew I had to get through this and do what I had to do no matter what the feelings and consequences.

Now I'm not telling you all this because I hate my sister because I don't, I'm telling you this because this is what happened at the time in my life and it's one of the many reasons why I love the bottle still. I'm sorry, liver, you're not getting off that lightly.

So, as we couldn't go on a week or two-week holiday because of my sister's wedding this year, we booked a short weekend to Denmark at the beginning of December 2018. It was brilliant and just want we needed.

In the next few pictures you can see we went to the Carlsberg factory and yes, I found a sausage dog in a shop. I don't like to disappoint my liver or my need for sausage objects. I had dabbled in not drinking this year with my endometriosis operation and something was niggling in my head telling me I should just give this poison up for good, you'd feel so much better without it. Just a few more drinkies in Denmark though...

In the meantime, throughout the year, we continue to go to Simon's parents for Sunday lunch, cause let's face it, who in their right mind wants to cook that shit on a Sunday when someone else is offering? I do really well with not drinking on a Sunday cause no one else is and, every so often, she cooks an amazing chocolate cake and I'm completely in love with cake now — ohhh noo, this is not good.

No, that's not why I have a muffin top people... it's definitely the endo.

Chapter 8
Booze 'The Shit Friend'

The week we moved into our new house, we had an electrician install two electric points in the garden just so we could get the lazy spa up. I mean only a crazy alcoholic would even consider that as a first option the week of moving in! It's not an essential item on anyone's list unless you want to get pissed in a hot bubbly outdoor bath and are concerned that the summer is almost over. Thank you, Mr Electrician.

We begin setting up the lazy spa, the water is going in so we leave it for a half-hour. We come back and what the f, there's a slight flood! Oh no, this can't be, it didn't survive the move.

Begin whaling on the floor: total disaster. And that, ladies and gentlemen, was the end of lazy spa drinking sessions. Although it only cost £300 ($402) to buy one, they had now gone up in price since our first purchase and we didn't really have an extra £500 ($670) to sink into a lazy spa- a pointless electrical point outside now, well its only good for the lawnmower and that does not help me with getting pissed, grrr. Plus our lawnmower is battery powered. Maybe it was a sign!

Thank god the pub is only down the road. So, our local is called the Barley Mow, and here it is...

It's one of those pubs that when you walk in the whole pub stops and turns round to see who it is. It's a local working man's pub, there are a few women but they're mainly behind the bar serving drinks.

Well, this is awkward being stared at but it's summer; I take a seat outside and let Simon go get the drinks in. Well, I'm sure you know what a few drinks do to you with no food inside... it makes you a great socialiser! A local guy comes up to us and starts having a chat and actually he is really lovely, we've bought the dogs with us as they are always a great conversation starter, he falls in love with Millie Moo who is sat in her dog bag and proceeds to take her around to everyone in the pub front garden. I obviously don't mind because it takes away me having to look after her and my main goal is drinking. It turns out to be a great night as we got to know a few locals and I got shitfaced — no change there then!

We make it a staple to go down every Friday and sometimes on a Saturday but we worked out that Friday was actually more fun as there is a younger crowd down there. There are basically two parts to this pub, the old man bit and the bit out the back which has darts and a pool table and is completely swarming with young people. Let's bear in mind that we're both 36 at this time and these guys are like 25/26, so a whole 10 years our junior. They were probably drunk at the time, but they politely say they didn't think we were that much older than them; I'm secretly amazed that we could fit in so well.

We do go into the old man bar because the toilets are in there and we eventually get to know the owner, who's a lovely chap, quite funny, and as he knows me now keeps asking me if I'm going for a poo every time he sees me going to the toilet — now that's my type of humour, yes very childish.

We do a lot of drinking with the young people and well, me being me, I never want the party to end so when it's almost closing time, I announce that we should take the party back to ours.

That went down well, a few drove their van/car round (don't ask!) and the rest of us staggered up the road to the local shop to grab some extra booze and then back to ours.

The parties we continue to have over a few months are epic, Simon has some amazing speakers that we hadn't really used so we set up Itunes every time, move the dining table and boom — a dance floor is created.

My kitchen and dining room are next to each other so this doesn't pose any problem getting to the all-important, amazing large American fridge for drinks. I don't have any photos because I started doing videos and books can't show them, but trust me the videos are all of us dancing and singing. The parties didn't generally end much before 4 am and luckily being in a detached house meant the neighbours didn't hear anything. This is turning out to be the perfect booze party house.

New Year was awesome, the pub put on an out of this world party, it was so busy they ran out of glasses to serve in so we had to have whatever they had available. My beloved bestie, Leila and her partner, John, joined us and I didn't know at this point that it would be one of the last times I would drink with my best friend.

Here we are — some New Year's Eve party pics. There's the obligatory crazy face required along with some classy drinking out of a bottle and swearing from John.

So you can see we basically had a lot of parties in our house and pub trips over six months, the light bulb moment came on 5th January 2019 when I woke up from one of our epic parties and I literally had enough of feeling like death warmed up every weekend, plus not actually doing anything other than drinking. I don't know why I, all of a sudden, had this thought because I knew that's what I'd been doing since forever but for some reason, that weekend, it resonated with me more.

I figured I have to take stock of my life and start doing things differently; I mean no one else is going to sort my life out but me. All I am doing is drowning my sorrows and drinking myself to death, I have to try and deal with this utter trauma of not being able to have children and get on a good path otherwise there's no point in my life.

It's now 2019, I'm 36 and well aware my fertility is on the verge of shutting down for good — umm, image of a shopkeeper putting a closing down sticker on me uterus springs to mind. So, after some discussions with the husband, we agree we should give this ruddy IVF another go — this was now a really good reason not to drink myself to death because one: I can't afford booze and IVF together and two: booze and IVF don't mix.

Now the best thing about Simon is that he's happy for me to do IVF as many times as I like, despite the cost, and also he's happy if I don't want to do it ever again. Basically, he's happy as long as I'm happy. We agree we can do this shit again and trot off to a clinic in Southampton which is quite a way, but their sister hospital is in the private clinic ten minutes away from us, so that will work perfectly for all the ruddy appointments in the coming months again.

In the meantime, I'm struggling with this forever concept of not drinking; if you've ever tried to give up drinking, you'll realise it's not easy when you've been drinking for, basically, your entire adult life.

You kinda have to rewire your brain into a different route. So rather than going down the crappy M25 (a horrible busy motorway for my American friends) where it's all congested and polluted and full of idiots doing the same journey, you need to veer off and go down a beautiful country road track, admittedly it's full of potholes but that's ok. They're just bumps in the road for this journey and eventually, there are no potholes and you travel down this amazingly free, clear road full of flowers on each side and there are a few cars on the way, but guess what, they're friendly and polite travellers, not reckless arseholes – that's what my journey of coming off the booze has been like. I don't want to follow the crowd anymore; I'm making my own way and guess what? It's more beautiful than I ever thought possible.

This journey takes some time because you should take the easy route back on to the M25 mainly because you know it like the back of your hand, whereas you've no idea where this country road takes you. It could be a load of bollox for all you know.

I can't say I didn't fall down any potholes on the way, because I did. I did three weeks and then thought, wow I know I can stop whenever I like so that's cool, I can go back. As soon as I had a morning with an epic hangover again, I despised the booze even more — that country road is starting to look like a great new short cut: woopie.

Booze is like having an enemy with you all your life who you thought was your friend. We've all had one of those friends that treat you like shit, not a proper friend but he/she is always there when you go out encouraging you to make shit decisions. So, I call my booze hound who is obviously in my head — 'the shit friend.'

Just stop and think about this. Have you ever tried to abstain or give up from drinking? If you look at the science of alcohol you wouldn't ever pour the stuff down your throat but it's okay because society's brainwashing says you can mix the toxic poison with something that tastes mildly okay like tonic or lemonade or coke. So basically, you really just want a nice flavoured drink, hence why they now do berry-flavoured gin or whatever. No one in their right mind would drink neat gin — yuck, it tastes like hairspray!

Anyway, I challenge you to not drink just for two weeks and if you can't do that my friend, you have a problem. The problem is fear, fear of the unknown, fear that you will feel different, fear that you won't enjoy it. The people who have a fear will say "I can do that, but I don't need to, I enjoy drinking". Okay so why not try something different? see if your life gets better and improves even more without drinking? The people who are addicted won't like this suggestion; they cannot see how not drinking could possibly be better. How do you know if you don't try though?

What I learnt is you cannot — I repeat, you can't tell yourself you're giving up forever. What you need to do is set a reasonable goal, say 100 days. When you get there, set another goal of 100 days. If you get to the 100 days and can't be arsed to do it anymore and are gagging to have a drink, then that's okay because you know what: you did it, you made it to 100 days and you may well want to try again in the future. As they say, get back on the horse.

And here I am getting back on a horse — literally. Yes, I love horse riding but sadly I can't keep it up because I'd have to sell my house and everything in it to afford to go on one bloody riding lesson.

Here's the thing, right, I found that finding a non-alcoholic drink that you like is a great way to stop 'the shit friend' from wanting you to consume booze. I stayed away from pubs for a good few months and that was quite easy in the end because I was consumed with doing IVF. When we did go out for a social with family, decaf coffee and non-alcoholic beer were my go-to drinks.

I'm not going to lie; it's hard to watch everyone having a drink but what I found the most helpful was, not going out for about a month just so I could get this sucker under some sort of control. It was only then that I could slowly introduce venturing out again. It wasn't often but when I did, I organised during the week meals out with friends which meant they either had to drive or only had one. I found that as long as I stipulated at the beginning of the evening that I wouldn't be drinking tonight then that set the mood and everyone followed suit. I then found I had some extremely meaningful evenings out with friends and guess what? I remembered the entire night and made it home all by myself and I didn't wake up feeling like death and broke.

If you're serious about getting back at the 'shit friend' and eliminating him from your friendship group entirely, don't expect it to be easy. I had many a time where I just went 'ohh, for Christ's sake I give up,' and then I had a glass of wine — great, back to day one! The more I kept on trying to do this the better at it I got, I knew I would feel better without 'shit friend' it was just re-learning to live my life again that was the difficult part- yes down that country road you remember? I seem to be constantly learning how to re-live my life a different way!

Saturday's used to be trying to get up and nurse the Friday night hangover, then we get to about 2 pm on a Saturday and be like well it's clearly beer o'clock so we'd crack one open and then depending on the level of drunkenness, make our way down to the Barley Mow for more consumption. Fuck dinner, I had lunch anyway but if we get hungry later, I'll have to chuck some crappy freezer pizza on or something. Oh yeah, the only annoying thing about living in a village out of town is delivery of junk food has come to a halt — what the fuck? These delivery companies are missing out on a lot of drunks who want a kebab or pizza at ridiculous o'clock, pfff idiots.

I was so used to getting home from work on a Friday and being like, yes let's get showered and ready and get down the pub which we both loved to do with the dogs. When I gave up the 'shit friend,' for me it was- what the hell do I do with all this spare time now? Our life was so entwined with going down the pub or anything to do with alcohol that this not-drinking was all so new and scary. So I'd say definitely be prepared to think about what you want to do with your time.

Simon loves computer gaming and so consumes himself with this on a Friday. I decided that Fridays would become my 'girls night in' — with the sausage dogs obviously. We would get home and have a nice dinner (questionable with my cooking skills), then watch a bit of 'us' TV (things we record that we can both enjoy), then Simon goes up to his room to play computer games with his friends online. You basically need to make a new routine and do something that you enjoy doing. If your trigger night is Friday, save that film you recorded to watch and watch it then.

Get yourself some popcorn/chocolate, your fav soft drink and go for it.

I found that organising my weekend with what I'm going to do before it even arrived, made getting through the first stages bearable when the 'shit friend' would rear its head. What you need to do, is think back to what hobbies or activities you used to do before you took up drinking. Maybe you like horse riding like I do, or tennis or art — now is the time to book yourself that lesson and bam — that's your Saturday morning sorted so you can't drink Friday anyway! Why not go bowling with your partner or with friends on Saturday night: bam you don't have to drink because you'll drive there. Make yourself the designated driver and that way you can't drink.

Now don't get me wrong, it took me some time to actually get into the hobbies I now enjoy. I resisted doing them for some time. I was just angry I had to do something else other than drinking so I'd start them and get bored and 'shit friend' would be like "Ummm put that crap down, go to the shop and get that cold, crisp bottle of wine you want," in my head I am like, "No, no, no fuck you, I won't do what you tell me."

Oh yeah, I can highly recommend (if you have space) a separate room each, as you know we have a four-bed house with no little fat sprogs in it so why the hell not have our own rooms? I can tell you; it's been so lovely being able to sleep in peace without someone snoring in your ear. We still pop over to one another's for some 'quality' time but I mean come on, all you do is sleep and when you're asleep you've no idea if anyone is lying next to you or not so fuck it — I'm off, see you in the morning. There are many nights where we do sleep in the same room but we mix it up so it's not stale.

Sorry, I digressed there... anyway....

I don't think a lot of people realise the amount of sugar lurking in alcohol. First of all, you will initially lose a bit of weight and the beer belly should flatten down — winner. Secondly, other sugar products are going to become your new best friend for a while. Yes, you may well gain a bit of weight back because of sugar intake but just watch what you are shoving in ya gob. I mean I haven't given up chocolate or sweets (candy for my American friends) but, fucking hell I'm not giving up everything, come on! Be prepared to have a need for sugar for some time. You may be lucky and not have this problem (I hate you) but all I'm saying is just be aware.

Other benefits of not drinking: your face looks less puffy, your skin and hair improve, your taste improves... you get it, you just start feeling like how a normal human should feel but you've never really remembered the experience because you started drinking when you were god knows how young.

I'd say after about a year of not drinking, I still love my sugar but I do know I'm replacing that lost sugar that was in my alcohol so because I'm aware of this, I'm now in control of what sugar I'm consuming. I limit a coffee and cake outing to once every few weeks and I only eat a small bit of dark chocolate every other day. So this is way less than the alcohol I was chucking down me neck. I combine my chocolate eating with making sure I do an hour walk with the dogs for exercise once a day so it's fine, shut up everyone (justified!).

Here's another thing I didn't realise when I gave the 'shit friend' up. You also lose relationships with people. Those 'friends' you used to go out drinking with, well you find they don't call you anymore. As you're not drinking, you've been thrown into the 'boring' pile. Excuse me I am not boring; you are the boring one because your life revolves around drink — ha suck on that.

You also need to be aware that relationships within your family will change. Perhaps you were used to going for a Prosecco with your mum every Saturday afternoon or a pint with ya dad. For me, this part was difficult because in our old house in Farnborough my mum would come round on weekends stay over and we would sit in the garden or sitting room and consume Prosecco together chatting away. This part was scary because now I'm giving up the booze, I don't have that connection we both had with alcohol anymore and I didn't know how to approach it because my mum loves a vino. I just had to not let it cloud my giving up booze venture and just hope we could do coffee and cake instead together; actually, that is what we do now and if we drink, I will have a non-alcoholic version.

Think of it like the baby thing, as in everyone (society) expects you to find a partner, settle down, buy a house, get married and have children. The End. Society, well, everyone, don't expect or know how to deal with the part where you don't have children.

So take the above but for drinking — you dabble in alcohol throughout your teenage years, you can finally have a drink at 18 (21 for my American friends) and in fact, it's celebrated that you do (society and everyone expect this of you), your parents encourage you to do this and your friends, you go to pubs and clubs with friends, you drink throughout your entire life. The End.

What society and everyone don't expect or know how to deal with is the part where you give up drinking... they can't comprehend a life without it and don't get it. Well, she/he must be some sort of weirdo!

If a smoker is an addict, it's blamed on the cigarettes, and society labels cigarettes as poison, it's not good for you and there are nicotine patches and chews available in chemists to help you give up.

If it's someone who's addicted to heroin or another equally high-end nasty drug, the drug is blamed; plus, there are clinics you can go to for help and an alternative drug to help you come off of whatever it is.

So, hang on a minute, why do people see the person who drinks alcohol as the problem, rather than the alcohol itself? Oh yeah, I know why! Because most people on this planet consume alcohol so it can't possibly be alcohol's fault. Wake up people, alcohol is a drug and a poison just the same as cigarettes and heroin/other drugs; everyone is susceptible to its grasp, for some reason when alcohol turns you into an alcoholic, they are seen as incapable and weak for not moderating the poison — this concept seems quite a bizarre way to think.

It's funny that we drink to celebrate, to relax, when we're angry and when we're sad and commiserating — so basically, we drink during all our emotions and we get used to it.

For example, Uncle Bob has died... oh, let's have a drink and celebrate his life. Then Uncle Bob's wife is on her own after the funeral and she starts to drink to numb the pain of this traumatic life event to try and deal with her loss. She does it in secret and hides it well and no one suspects her. She becomes more of a recluse and depressed, more fearful and anxious; I'm just explaining this as a reminder to not let anyone who has had a traumatic life event slip under the radar no matter how small an event you think it is, it could be huge to that person and send them over the edge.

We seem to use alcohol as a way of coping in every aspect of our lives. We think we have control of this alcohol moderation thing but you can so very easily slip into consuming more than society expects you to — well I didn't know there was a bloody etiquette for getting pissed!

People don't understand why you can't control what you drink because they can so why can't you? Well, I'm so sorry I had a traumatic life event... well more than one traumatic event and hit the bottle — give me a break! Perhaps you eat too much or exercise excessively or have a shopping addiction or work too much or smoke or take drugs. Everyone has their vices, mine just happened to be alcohol.

I've told you I used to smoke, well, I smoked about twenty a day for ten years. It's disgusting now I think about it. I read the incredible Allen Carr's The Easy Way. After reading it about eight times, I finally gave up smoking. I guess you could say I was brainwashed into it but hey, I'm a proud non-smoker and have been for about 15 years so brainwash me all you want on that one, I'm just glad I'm not spending money on sucking on an exhaust anymore.

I looked up Allen Carr again and he has done a book called 'Stop Drinking Now' which I purchased and it was very good. It has helped me to see things more clearly. With giving up smoking, people are amazed you've done it and are so happy for you and praise you and celebrate it. It's an amazing feeling and you feel like you've really achieved something big. You're no longer the leper of society.

I'll give you a heads up, you don't get any of that when you give up drinking. Everyone thinks you're boring and you become the leper of society; then they avoid you because in their head being an alcoholic is drinking a bottle of neat vodka in a paper bag on the street, so why do you need to give up. You get the comments of "Can't you just moderate?", "Can't you just have one?", "Can't you just drink at weekends?", "You can't give up, that's boring", "What the heck are you going to do instead?" "How can you go out now?".

So, when I get asked these questions, I just look at these people and think wow, just wow. These people have never even thought of what the other side looks like; I'd love to show them but they ain't interested. I'd also like to explain to them that the same as with smoking or overeating, you just get to a point where what you've consumed isn't enough, so you drink more to get that high feeling. Then you start drinking more often because it's never enough to block out your emotions — like overeaters, smokers or drug addicts. I am an all-or-nothing girl and I have to take the nothing otherwise I'm gonna end up in a gutter drinking vodka out of a paper bag.

Can I also just say that people who have given up the 'shit friend' can't *ever* just have one. It doesn't work like that, if you have one, you're keeping the 'shit friend' alive in your head and feeding it. Do you know what happens when you have just one? That's right, you have two the next time you go out, and then you're on to three the next time. It spirals very quickly and before you know it, you're back to drinking two bottles of vino every night — back to day one then! It's a bit like smoking:

would you ever just have one fag? No, you wouldn't because you've given up.

The thing is, when you take on giving up a demon, you need to pack your suitcase full of stuff to bash him or her over the head with. Think of it like becoming an exorcist, I'm sure they don't go anywhere without their bible and cross. So, you also shouldn't do this journey without filling your suitcase full of sober goodies so you can tell the 'shit friend' you don't want him/her to come on holiday with you anymore.

I filled mine with books about how to give up drinking, books about people who had given up booze, blogs about people giving up and I joined Facebook communities. I have to keep opening that suitcase and getting the odd book or blog out to bash that 'shit friend' away. He lurks about but I can tell you he doesn't visit very frequently anymore; he must be annoying the shit out of someone else — ahh, I can relax. Shit no, he's back, get a book out!!

The point is, you will have to keep getting your suitcase out just to remind yourself how far you've come and that you won't be going back to that 'shit friend' anymore. I can recommend a few bits in my suitcase:

- The Sober Revolution by Sarah Turner and Lucy Rocca (Book)
- The Unexpected Joy of Being Sober by Catherine Gray (Book and Facebook)
- The Sober Diaries by Clare Pooley (Book)
- Stop Drinking Now by Allen Carr (Book)
- My Sober Compass Inner Circle (Facebook)
- Give Up Alcohol (Facebook)

- Soberocity (Blog)
- The Fix (Blog)
- Sober Courage (Blog)
- Club Sober (Blog)
- Drunky Drunk Girl (Blog)

You get it, and there are a lot more, all you have to do my friends is type it on google or Facebook or frequent a book shop. Just immerse yourself with sober people and you'll get that connection again with people who just 'get it'.

As I said, people think of drunks as a person on the street with bad clothes, bad hair, drinking out of a bottle in a paper bag. Now, do you not think that person had a decent life before he/she ended up like that? Do you not think that maybe, just maybe the drinking got out of control, they lost their job, family, and home, and are now on the street? It takes a lot to get to this stage; you can be a functioning drunk and a high society posh toff drunk before you get to that stage but goddamit, I know I would have been there if I hadn't acted. Just take a look at how alcohol affects your emotions, it's called bad decision juice for a reason. Alcoholism is a real thing and it's not something to be taken lightly. Think about Uncle Bob's wife!

I was embarrassed that I was using alcohol to drown out my emotions and I couldn't go to anyone because they all drink and wouldn't get it. I am living a life I really didn't want to live and drinking made me out of control, whereas now I'm not drinking, I feel perfectly in control. I have no control over my fertility and never will, but I can at least have some control over other aspects of my life and alcohol is one.

So, the next time you meet someone or know someone who has given up the 'shit friend' just give them a pat on the back and make them see that it's something to celebrate. Don't treat them like they're wrong for what they've achieved because it's quite a feat to give up a demon that you know society won't be accepting of. Plus bring me a chocolate cake, I need one!

Chapter 9
IVF again… are you sure?

Woooohoooooo! I've bagged that 'shit friend' up and taken him down to the dump. So, we're now about March 2019 and I'm about to do the expensive self-funded IVF treatment… Oh Jesus, let's do this. I have to tell my boss that I'm doing IVF and I have to make up the time again. If only there was some sort of government work policy in place for people going through this at work. I believe it's as many as 1 in 8 women and 1 in 10 men who have a problem with fertility, so something should be in place!

We head down to the clinic in Southampton for our first

appointment. I'm anxious because this is a new clinic. We get through the talk, they take our blood and send us on our way with a lot of paperwork, yet again!

The next time we come back to Southampton we hand in our mountain of paperwork and they've obtained our IVF records from our first rounds. They perform an internal scan on me and we sit down to discuss things. The first thing she says is, "From your scan, I can see as well as the endometriosis you also have adenomyosis, do you know what that is?" So now I'm thinking, "Christ what is this 'osis' thing, another bloody disease to stop me from reproducing?" I then say, "Well I know I have Endometriosis."

She explains that adenomyosis and endometriosis aren't the same condition. Although they can occur together, endometriosis is when endometrial cells (the lining of the uterus) are located outside the uterus. Adenomyosis is when these cells grow into the wall of the uterus. To top it all off nothing cures it. Oh great, just great, so it's like double endo pain — happy birthday/Christmas to me forever.

This round of IVF sounds like it's going to be a hard, long process and very expensive now with all my bloody added internal diseases. So, we have an extended meeting where she explains that I will need to go on their 'Endometriosis protocol' which has slightly different drugs. There are also a list of 'add-ons' you can have, I can think of two from the list- endo glue (helps with sticking the egg to your lining) and an endometrial scratch (they use an implement to scratch your lining, helps the egg with blood supply when they implant it back).

We also have to pay upfront for the drugs and the operation, so we're now approximately £7,500 ($9,300) lighter in our wallet (wobbly bottom lip as I hand over my card). All I could think is this is one bloody expensive baby that I've not even got yet!

These people who can just get pregnant have no idea how good they have it because they don't have to pay to get pregnant in the first place and **if I do get** pregnant, I'm now thinking how the hell am I going to afford to feed the poxy thing (joking, I will do, but bugger me sideways, the clinics are a rip-off).

I opt for the scratch and what is also not lovely is that I have to have a special injection which the clinic has to administer so at the same time I have the injection I collect my chemist set — I mean IVF drugs.

The doctor advises that I need to wait to come on my period, call the clinic and book my 'injection' (which they do in-house) about a week later…don't quote me on this, it could have been longer but these drugs mess with your memory!

So, we trot off to our next appointment to have my special injection a week or so later, this time in the sister clinic near us, handy. Oh, balls… I'm not the best with injections (you'd think I'd be okay after so many) but this sucker is huge. I have to lie on the bed to have it, she grabs/pinches my muffin top and jabs it in — well we should have warned the water company at this point because I'm in floods of tears… ouch you fucking bitch that really hurt (said in my head).

Simon, bless him, doesn't know how to take it but gives me a massive hug and takes me for a coffee after. Ouchy, my poor muffin top.

They did give me a lesson and a sheet to tell me exactly when to take my drugs and how much to put in. This time the injections were different, they were pre-filled pens. Now, I'm not speculating here, but is this because we paid for it? The last set of drugs I had to bloody mix myself! I'm not complaining because this is way easier and takes away the anxiety of getting the mixing wrong, all I have to do with these bad boys is set the limit on the pen and ta-da. Amazingly I didn't even have to have lots of blood tests either! Winner.

I had to do about three weeks of injections day and night then I went for an internal exam to see whether the eggies are juicy enough to be extracted.

Basically, the layman's science is the eggs have to get to a certain size before they can be taken out, I believe it is about 15-22mm. Well, bloody hell mine aren't complying with the drugs so right there and then they had to give me another prescription of a week's worth of injections… ka-ching for them! Oh, it's only another £650 ($807)!! I mean for Christ's sake as if this wasn't expensive enough.

I've come to the sad realisation that we're not going on a holiday for at least two years now! This is ironic because you actually do need a holiday after you've gone through all of this just to get away and relax and have some 'you' time like anyone does after a trauma in their life — ha-ha forget that love, it's not happening unless some rich mofo takes pity on you.

Anyway, so after another bout of drugs me eggs are finally juicy enough to come out. The operation is booked for lunchtime the next day. I had to take a final injection which is the one in the fridge and I think it was about 24 hours before the operation. I had to go into the clinic in Southampton to have my operation egg removal and poor Simon had to do the 'deed' (world's most expensive wank!). I'm very woozy coming round from anaesthetic and me ovaries feel a bit bruised so I go home to rest. Now I must have three day's of rest and luckily, I had the op on a Friday so chill time for the weekend. "Simon get me tea," "Simon get me chocolate," "Simon get me cake,"… poor Simon.

The clinic called me in the afternoon after the operation to say they retrieved four eggs (that's one less than last time) bit disappointed but I'm getting old in the fertile years now and I do have a low ovarian reserve. Anyway, I'm just happy to get one out!

The eggs and sperm have a party again and we get a call over the week every two days to tell us if they have survived and, if they have grown… well the following day after the operation we were informed that one had died (sad face) but the other three are growing. They basically want them to start dividing and growing and when they have divided enough, they call it a blastocyst stage which is when they can either safely freeze your egg(s) or transfer them to your uterus. You people who can get preggers never find out about all this stage because it's happening behind your closed doors: lucky fuckers!

By day four we had lost another egg but we had two eggs that had got to blastocyst stage— woohoo rejoice singe alleluia. So, we opt to freeze one and have one put back. I've got a half-full bladder again and this time the transfer is different; they use an ultrasound to see on the screen where they are putting the egg in, very clever but hurry the fuck up or I'm going to wee all over this poor surgeon! It does take a good six or seven minutes before they get it exactly right. They take an ultrasound picture of your little egg for you to take home; aww never had an ultrasound pic before, this must be what pregnant people feel like: overjoyed.

I'm so happy the procedure is done, I'm told to move slowly and take it really easy for four days, so basically just lie on the sofa and do nothing again — no hot baths or hot showers, no lifting anything, no walking or exercise and eat healthily. Ohh bugger I was gonna get a Burger King on the way home, that's that one out then! I go home with my little egg picture feeling all positive and happy.

As before, I've got a test to do on an exact day, which is twelve days after transfer. Ohh the wait is excruciating. My work colleagues know about my IVF at this point and they are all routing for me and actually are very helpful with not letting me lift anything or do anything I shouldn't and keeping my mind sane.

Test day: I've taken the day off work because with either outcome I'm going to need a day at least to process it. Ok, so I've woken up at 5 am, actually I was awake before that praying and wishing and feeling sick at what the outcome will be. I can't wait any longer, I pee on the stick (gross) and wait for the result.

FUCK ME SIDEWAYS... OMG, OMG, OMG I'M PREGNANT! I'm so excited I can't believe this has actually happened. Ok calm down, calm down. When it was open, I phoned the clinic and they said they would phone me back.

Whilst we waited for our call, we trotted off down to Southampton for a bit of shopping and lunch. The clinic phoned me when we were down there and said, "You've done the test on the wrong day, it's tomorrow; you'll have to do another test tomorrow." I said, "Sorry but I haven't, I've done it on the day you put on my sheet." (I'm panicking now thinking it's a false positive). The lady comes back a few minutes later (whilst I'm feeling sick) and says, "Oh sorry, you're right it was today, congratulations. We will need to book your six-week scan which is in two weeks' time where you can see the heartbeat."

Well as you can imagine, I'm itching to tell the whole world that I am pregnant, but we agree we should wait until the 12-week scan and then tell people just in case: like everyone else does.

It was May 2019; we had the six-week scan and see our little nugget and a heartbeat — how incredibly precious this moment is, and I'm smiling from ear to ear holding Simon's hand. The next scan is booked for eight weeks, but in the meantime, we go on holiday to Cornwall (seaside town) in a static caravan park with our dogs.

It takes about 3 ½ hours to get there and then… "Simon we've forgotten my suitcase — fuck that's got all my fucking drugs in!" OMG, complete meltdown panic, we're going to have to drive all the way home. Some frantic searching later and we realised one of us had taken it out and already put it in the caravan — mini heart attack under control. I have to keep taking them horrible pessaries and another oral drug at certain times of the day and you have to rest for 30 minutes just to chill out and let the drugs sink in. That holiday was a fab break away, all of us together and finally our little family on the way.

We came back and had our eight-week scan; the little muffin had grown, it was amazing and we got another scan picture. I mean it's only a little dot but it's our dot! We decided we would just go and have a quick look around a baby store at all the baby stuff just because we could and to get an idea of costs. Holy cow, I didn't realise a buggy could cost that much! We were both feeling all happy and kinda like this is surreal and can't believe this is finally happening.

I had calculated that actually our 12-week scan was going to roughly fall on Father's Day (21 June in UK). This was perfect because the best Father's Day present will be a 12-week scan picture in his card. Oh, I cannot wait, it's going to be so exciting. I also can't wait to start baby clothes shopping with mum... oh, I need to calm down as all sorts can happen between now and then.

We then got about halfway through the week, almost at nine weeks, I went to the toilet and I had a dot, yes, a dot of blood. The smallest dot ever but I completely panicked; it was a Sunday, and the clinic wasn't open. I called the early pregnancy unit at the local hospital in a state, they said not to worry because it was quite common, but they can do a scan to be sure and booked me in for the Wednesday morning — phew!

It was the longest wait ever and no other symptoms on my part either thank god. We get to the early pregnancy unit on Wednesday, the sonographer does an internal scan, and she says the worst thing I wanted to hear, "I'm really sorry, I can't detect a heartbeat, I'll get a doctor just to confirm." Simon is looking at me and I look at him. He just squeezes my hand and I say, "I knew it was too good to be true."

The doctor confirms what she'd said. She looks at me and says, "Are you okay?" I hold it together and just say "yes, what is the next stage?" She gets a leaflet out, hands it to me and explains I can either just wait for the miscarriage to occur itself, they can give me a drug to speed up the miscarriage or they can book me in for a removal in the hospital." Well, I don't really want to see my baby in a toilet thank you, so I opt for the removal in hospital. She books me in for Friday.

I came out of the hospital and broke down; my dreams and hopes for the future have just been shattered in one three-minute appointment. My world has just ended, what did I do to deserve this? Was it because I looked around Mother Care, was it because I thought about enjoying this with my mum and dad? This can't be true; they must have it wrong! I've just spent thousands of pounds to have this terrible outcome; someone call

Kleenex, their stocks might deplete imminently.

That afternoon was a complete blur; we went home, and my wonderful husband Simon called everyone that needed to know. Starting with my work, I was booked off for two weeks from the Friday, but I wasn't going to be going in anyway, I was distraught.

Friday, the procedure day was awful; it took ages to get seen to as there seemed to be no one about. I was in the same hospital wing that gave me the bad news a few days ago and to top it all off, I was sat on a hospital bed next to a pregnant young woman — bloody great!

I wasn't allowed to eat anything since the night before, so I was fucking starving. I had to be fitted in around any accidents and emergencies, so I didn't go down for my operation until about 1:30 pm. The preparation nurse came round gave me a gown and explained what will happen — basically it sounded like they were going to use a Dyson. To be honest, I wasn't listening a great deal; I just wanted the procedure to be done so I could go home and eat.

At 1:30 pm I walk down to the anaesthetist room and lay on the bed whilst four doctors whizzed around me, getting all sorts of instruments and things out and others are sticking needles in my arm then comes the gas over my face and then one, two... threeee... I'm out.

I come round in a massive room that has other people in who are also waking up from operations and being monitored. The nurse leans over me and reassures me everything went well and as soon as a certain amount of time has passed, they'll wheel me up to a room.

I get wheeled up to a private room an hour later and panic because Simon isn't there. They go and get him and we have a massive cuddle and a cry. This is gross but I have what I can only describe as a river of blood like in the bible; it's scary and I feel like my innards are falling out. The nurse comes to help me clean up and assures me this is normal. I lay in the bed all numb and feeling overwhelmingly sad.

Simon deals with all the calls and texts we're getting and also gets me a sarnie and a soft drink because the ruddy hospital offered me nothing! Now, most people would be let out after an hour or so, but not me, oh no. I always have low blood pressure when I have operations, so they keep me in until it's back to normal and so I'm not allowed out until about 8 pm. I'm completely exhausted and can't wait to get home.

When we do get home, we just go to bed and hold each other all night... all the drama and the drugs knock me out.

The only thing that annoyed me about the whole miscarriage was what others say a few months after the event. I got things like "I had several miscarriages before I had my children." In my mind, I thought, "Great thank you for that but you don't understand my position because you have children and I forgot we have exactly the same body down to our fingerprints." Bloody idiot. I mean come on, every single one of us is unique, your miscarriage and my miscarriage were different eggs in a different womb — it's not the bloody same! Plus, you probably don't have low ovarian reserve, bloody endometriosis, adenomyosis and didn't spend thousands of pounds to feel this shit! Jesus — I sound angry because I am!

The next common one was, "At least you got pregnant and know your body can do it." Oh yes, that's perfect, thank you for that helpful insight; I forgot I hadn't been trying for several years with a load of failed IVFs and no natural pregnancy every month. That pregnancy of mine was a one-off and very expensive, there is NO, I repeat, NO guarantee that will ever happen again.

Do people actually think before they open their mouths? How about just saying something like, "I know you are hurting right now; I won't pretend I understand but you can talk to me about your experience and I will listen and be here for you. I'm here to cheer you up if you want me to," – that's all we need people, it's not that difficult.

We don't need this dialogue where you tell us about thingy down the bloody road who had five miscarriages and ten rounds of IVF but then had two beautiful children in the end... believe it or not, we don't want to hear about thingy, we don't give a rat's arse about thingy or any of the others. We want our problem to be validated and heard and you not to give us any 'solution' that you think might help; do you not think we've tried and thought of everything?

We get that you're trying to give us hope and make us see the lighter side of things but honestly, just don't. Just say the words I've said above and your friend or family member will be elated that you care enough to want to sit, listen and cuddle them and acknowledge their trauma.

Plus put the kettle on and make a good cup of tea! Don't forget the chocolate cake though or there will be war.

Chapter 10
A magpie called Bert #bekind

I will explain the title; Bert is a magpie Simon and I seem to see when we drive or walk down this particular road that is near us. The old saying goes 'one for sorrow, two for joy, etc, etc.' All the way through our IVFs or any procedures driving to any appointments we would see Bert on his own and I'd always say to Simon "oh no, one for sorrow." He got sick of me saying it so one day he said, "Don't be so fucking crazy that myth is a load of old bollox, I've decided that Bert is not one for sorrow anymore, he is just Bert and if we see another, we call her Sally." His reasoning was we can't have any more bad times because the magpie is called Bert, now, he was very wrong... I basically think Bert is a bit of an arsehole, but don't tell Simon though.

Whilst all these bad times are going on, Simon is having a really hard time at work dealing with a big office move (he works in IT), so sadly the week after the miscarriage operation he tries his best to get home early or take time off to be with me. I can't stop wailing; all I want is for him to hold me and tell me it will be okay; I don't want anything or anyone else. I'm sat at home with the dogs cuddling on the sofa feeling so alone and just dealing with bouts of uncontrollable crying. People call me and send me flowers and chocolates and cards which was overwhelming and lovely, but I just want Simon.

Our best mate, Del, suggested we both come out to Spain with him to stay in his mum's villa for four days. I jump at the chance, so we book a four-day break for the following week. Sadly, with Simon's work it's all we could get and we really both needed a week or two just together, but it was just not possible for him.

So here we are on the plane! Up, up and away.

Here is the beautiful villa. We had the ground floor bedroom and bathroom. Sadly, I wasn't allowed in the pool due to my operation, but I dangled my feet in and it was delightful.

Even though it was a short break, it was just what we needed. Del and his mum were the only ones who reached out to physically help us get away during our time of absolute despair, grief and need. With all the money we'd spent on IVF we were broke but luckily, we only had to pay for flights. Del's mum looked after us, she fed us every day and took us to places to take our minds off the miscarriage.

We all went out for a lovely meal at the end of the break which was on us as a thank you, and I still can't thank them enough. They were like little angels that came down at the right time. They're the true essence of #bekind.

Here we all are on our final meal out.

So, we get back to the UK and reality kicks in. I can't stop crying and just feel utterly sad and like my life is not even worth living. I mean what is the point of me? If I was a cow I'd have been put down by now because I can't produce a calf and milk: useless. Yes, I'm aware that's not a way to think but it's true in the animal world!

After my two weeks is up, I'm back at work and feeling awful. Work colleagues are kind and also can't believe that this happened but feed me chocolate and tea and I get stuck into some work to numb the pain and try to take my mind off things.

A few weeks go by and I end up having a few rows with work colleagues and I just know I'm a shell of my former self and I am angry and upset a lot of the time. I had asked my manager if I could perhaps be given fewer duties, purely because I only do a four-day week and the others do a five-day week so it would have made sense to swap some roles and would have helped me out with all I was going through to ease the pressure. Despite my pleas, this didn't happen and sadly, I was told this wasn't going to be the case as the department was too busy. So basically, it was a put up with the shit you already do or quit your job scenario. I'm now stuck between a rock and a hard place. It's either I stay and completely crash and burn, or fuck off!

Before I'd gotten pregnant there was a course that people were doing at work, but I didn't take it because I thought, what's the point I'm gonna be a mum and be off for nine months so it would be a waste of their money. Well as that hadn't happened and I wasn't going to be put on lesser duties, I asked if I could now take this course and they were happy for me to do this. It took me about three weeks and what do you know, I passed with a distinction — 100%! Bloody hell I've never got that good of a result at anything.

Whilst I was taking this course, it was about a few days before I finished it, I just thought to myself is this really what I want to do for the rest of my life?

I mean seriously, it's really hard work trying to squeeze five days' work into a four-day week, and I'm struggling with my personal life a lot. Yeah, heads up, four days is great, but you end up doing the same amount of work as five days anyway. There were some people that I just wasn't getting on with at work and it became horrible to think I spend most of my life with these people so I had a big decision to make.

I was continually coming home just sobbing to Simon, he could see I was massively struggling and really hating my job and my job couldn't help me ease the pressure because they were too busy. I was turning into an angry, horrible mess and I'm sure Simon will agree, I wasn't nice to live with.

Simon had had enough of me feeling like this so he told me I need to hand my notice in. Now as lovely as that sounds, I just couldn't give the entire burden of house bills to Simon after everything else we've just been through, it seemed like a bitch thing to do. He was totally insistent and said I need time to chill out and besides, the dogs would like to have their mum around and that takes the pressure off him having to deal with them and the house chores.

Well, me being me, I couldn't leave my job without another job. I'd never not had a job in my life, I've always worked, even when I was at school. I'd been looking online at jobs to see if I could find anything near to me and a job for a carer came up in a private nursing home five minutes' drive from me. Perfect! It's a total change of career, I know I'm a kind caring person, so I need to give this a go and why not?

I get a call the next day after submitting my CV and head on down for an informal interview. She didn't see any reason not to offer me a position but said there would be training first; I was really happy about this and this meant I could hand in my notice!

The next day I go to work, I write out my notice and gingerly take it up to my boss. I'm totally shitting it cause I've just done the course, but I know I need to do this. I hand her my note she looks at it and then gives me a massive hug and says she completely understands why as I've been through a lot. I explain I just need a complete change and have found a job in a nursing home and she says she will give me a reference: wow that was scary, but I feel like a massive weight has been lifted. On Friday 6th September 2019 I said my goodbyes and left for good.

I started my new job at the end of September but I found that most of the staff were foreign and were talking in their own language; I gave it a week but I just couldn't cope with it, I just didn't understand the people that I was working with and I wanted it to be a lovely caring place to work where I could make new friends. I was the odd one out yet again and I felt even more alone. I realised I was just running away from dealing with my feelings and I obviously felt that a change of job would help me feel better, but it really didn't.

I got to work at the care home and carried on with my training, but I was so upset after just a morning working there, I started to panic and felt trapped and alone. I ran outside and called Simon to explain what happened and he just said, "Calm down, go get your things and just leave. You're not under contract so you can just tell them you can't do it and come home, I'd rather you looked after the dogs anyway, like I already said. You don't need to work."

I argued the point with him that I needed a job, but he was insistent that I leave so that's what I did. I've never felt so useless in my entire life.

I gave it my all but my emotions were just too strong to deal with from the miscarriage and so I grabbed my things, explained to the manager and then I sat in my car crying waiting for the tears to stop so I could drive home.

When I got home, I hugged the dogs and just sat on the sofa until my wonderful husband came home from work and reassured me that everything will be fine. Plus, we got a Nando's takeaway which always cheers me up. He told me there was no need to find another job, just chill out for a few months with the dogs as I've been through a lot. We'd already worked out he earns more than enough to cover everything with some left over so I can take my time deciding what I want to do, if anything.

I decided that I wanted to do our last frozen IVF round whilst I'm off and relaxed as this would be the perfect time and I don't have to find a job at the moment. So, we began our last round with our last egg. We had paid for the round and I was booked for the horrible scratch again and injection. I was beginning to calm down, taking the dogs for a walk every day and trying to enjoy the time off.

On Thursday 12th September I took the dogs up to the church as there's a beautiful walk behind it. We got about a quarter of the way and one of my dogs, Poppy, decided she didn't want to walk anymore. This was most unusual for Poppy because she is the 'proper' dog, never wants picking up and does her own thing. I called Simon and he came to meet us I wanted to see whether Poppy maybe wouldn't walk because Simon wasn't there with us but it wasn't that. She didn't seem herself all day and stayed in her bed.

Later that evening I noticed whilst she was lying on the sofa with me that her breathing seemed rather quick. I got my timer out and counted her breaths per minute, looked it up and noticed that it was higher than it should be. We agreed I would take Poppy to the vet the next day.

I managed to get an emergency appointment the morning of Friday 13th— great what a day to go to the vet! Poppy absolutely hates the vet so she was terrified; I had Millie Moo with me also which wasn't helping the matter she got anxious and was moaning.

The vet examined Poppy whilst I explained to her that she was constantly stopping on walks and was more tired than usual, plus her breathing was very fast at rest. She gave her the once over and stopped at her stomach area. She looked at me and said, "I can feel a melon-sized lump in her stomach, this will have to be operated on today."

I did say to the vet I did notice she was always a bit fatter than Millie Moo but every time we had come for a check-up with the nurse, the nurse always said

Poppy had put a bit of weight on. I couldn't understand because Millie Moo was staying the same weight and they ate and exercised the same, but I just didn't think anything of it and neither did the nurse. Poppy is a bigger dog then Millie Moo anyway, Never in a million years did I think something was growing inside her and I begin to feel horribly guilty; I started to think I could have asked about this before. Why didn't I notice it? I asked the vet what it could be, and she said the surgeon would call us once they have done an MRI and an x-ray to confirm things.

I left Poppy at the vets and on the drive home felt my heart beating so fast. OMG this can't be happening! I called Simon to explain and he was really upset and said he would come home at lunch. The vet called a short time later and explained that looking at the scans, they can confirm it looks like a cancerous lump growing in her spleen. They'll do an operation to remove the spleen today, but they won't be able to tell if it has spread until they go in. If it has spread, we may need to make a decision there and then whether to continue the operation or not; they'll call me in a few hours.

Jesus, fucking hell… what is going on with everything? I can't believe I'm dealing with yet more trauma, I can't cope with this I'm trying to remain calm but I'm just watching my phone the entire time for the vet to call and I feel sick. My baby is on the operating table, her life in their hands and Simon didn't even get to say a proper goodbye.

The vet calls after about two hours and explains that he went ahead and removed Poppy's spleen and he could see a very small amount of spreading to her liver. He said he thinks it's a hemangiosarcoma but they'll send it off to the lab to confirm this and decide on what treatment Poppy can have in a few weeks.

We go along to pick up Poppy and it's the best feeling to have her back in our arms again; we both weep and cuddle Poppy and Millie Moo all night.

Poppy makes a really good recovery over the next week and I spend a lot of time with her, taking her to lovely places and over to family so we can all enjoy her. I can't explain the feelings we both have for our dogs; they're like our children because we haven't been able to have any. They've been there for us for the last nine years; they've been through everything with us.

Two weeks later we got a call from the vet with Poppy's results. She explains that sadly it is a hemangiosarcoma which is an extremely aggressive cancer; she advised that without any treatment Poppy would have a life expectancy of four to six months. The treatment they can offer is with another surgery, which they can refer us to. It's about an hour away and it would be a chemotherapy treatment but, it's not like human chemo, it's very mild and does not hurt the dog. This may extend her life for another six months but they really didn't know for sure. The vet explained that we could contact them if we want to go ahead.

Another fucking worst day ever! Basically, being told my baby is dying, I felt physically sick; we only just had her ninth birthday last month!

We sat down that evening with the dogs and decided that it would be very selfish of us to put Poppy through chemo. She is nine years old and should technically live until fifteen or sixteen years old so we've only had her half her life. It's a heartbreaking decision to make but we decided to just let her live her life as happily as she can and we'll know when the time will come to make the decision to say goodbye.

At the end of September, we go away to a beautiful place called Malham Beck which is in the north of the UK with the dogs.

We stay in an amazing dog-friendly hotel called Beck Hall for a long weekend and explore the beautiful Yorkshire Dales and Lake District to get some family pics, as sadly we know this is our last holiday together. When we get home, we go to the beach as well; we try and spend as much time together at the weekends as possible.

This last month has been just wonderful spending every day with my gorgeous dogs, I'm so grateful for all the time with Poppy. We didn't get upset during this time as we were just hoping that she would be around for a good few months and we need to remain positive. We were hoping she would defy the odds of what the vet had said.

In remaining positive, we'd started our last IVF round; we had paid for it, so we had to continue. This time it was £3,000 ($3,768) for the frozen round and Simon's parents very kindly gave us massive financial help to keep going with it. I continued injections myself from home, there were no appointments in between to attend, thank god!

By the middle of November, our beautiful Poppy is now too tired to go on any walks and she's breathing heavily. Sadly, we're aware that a decision is going to have to be made and it's a lot sooner than the vet had predicted; we didn't have four to six months, we had her for exactly ten weeks. We decide that as Poppy hates going to the vet so much, we didn't want to make her last day anymore traumatic than it needed to be for any of us, so we book the vet to come out on 22nd November and they advise they will come out about lunchtime.

Simon has as much time as he can off with us that week. Family members who love Poppy come round to say their goodbyes and it's devastating to watch. We decide to take the dogs down to West Wittering beach as a last treat to get some lovely photos. It's a happy but truly sad day.

These are our last pictures of Poppy and us together. We had made a lot of videos for memories as well which we will treasure forever.

On the 22nd November 2019, a part of our hearts was ripped out as we held Poppy in our arms on our sofa whilst she quietly slipped away. We were allowed some time with her body to say our goodbyes and let Millie Moo also say goodbye. The vet took her body away and we both broke down.

We just couldn't believe another tragic event had taken another baby away again this year. This was truly the worst day of my entire life; I've never loved anything as much as I loved this little dog. We went to Simon's parents for the weekend as we just couldn't sit at home on the sofa where we'd said goodbye to Poppy.

I can truly say that I'm now not terrified of dying. Now I know that my Poppy is (I like to believe) somewhere in the next life and waiting for Simon, Millie Moo and me, it gives me comfort knowing that she will be there, and we will all be together again one day.

We couldn't stop the IVF despite having to deal with the trauma of saying goodbye to Poppy and so had a scan on Monday 25th November 2019 where they told me that my womb was now ready for the Transfer of the egg and they booked me in for Thursday 5th December 2019 for transfer day.

I wasn't feeling happy because of Poppy but all I could think of is maybe, just maybe this little egg will bring us some joy after such a tragic year. I tried to remain positive; losing Poppy hadn't quite totally sunk in so we were able to pull ourselves together to go and have this transfer.

After the transfer, I sat on the sofa all weekend and just generally chilled out over the next two weeks. Tuesday 17th December 2019 rolls around — test day again. I wake up early, for some reason I just have a feeling this hasn't worked… low and behold I was right.

That week the vet also called and said Poppy was ready to pick up; we picked up her little urn and sobbed our hearts out. This was really starting to hit home; my baby wasn't going to come back. All I could think of was I'm never going to get to see my baby Poppy grow old and look after her, hold her, take her places and enjoy my life with her ever again. My poor Millie Moo was without her sister and also grieving.

That was it, I was done with all this tragedy. I've lost a baby, quit my job, lost my Poppy dog and a fertilised egg all in one year. I'm totally done with 2019. In fact, 2019 has been the worst year on record, wouldn't you agree?

Here is my beautiful Poppy – miss her so, so much!

All I want to say is, just remember, everyone you meet is fighting a battle inside you know nothing about so be kind. ALWAYS. #bekind

The Butterfly

Someone once said, "I don't know how you do it."

I said, "I wasn't given a choice."

Chapter 11

Journeying Together

At the beginning of November 2019, before my beloved Poppy passed away, I was dabbling with thoughts of what job I could do but I didn't know what I wanted to do. I thought the best way to find out if I like something is to do some voluntary work.

I decided that maybe volunteering at the local nursery might be helpful for me in de-sensitising myself to being around children without getting upset. I mean the mums wouldn't be there, it would just be the kids which would be much better for me. There'd be no intrusive adult questions and conversations.

I approached the local nursery and sure enough, they were delighted. I dedicated a Tuesday morning every week. I was absolutely terrified when I first started, the anxiety going on in my head was crazy. What will the other people think of me because I don't have kids? Will they ask me lots of questions about my fertility problems? Will I be judged? Ahhhh! I can safely say after the first two sessions, I really started to enjoy myself, everyone was kind and understanding and no one judged me at all. I mean it wasn't without the questions but short sharp answers and getting on with the task in hand was the best way for me. The kids were great fun, I did lots of fun things and helped out with snacks and storytime. Strangely, this one day a week was really helping with my self-esteem and confidence levels because they'd been at an all-time low for some time because I didn't have a job, my family and friends are miles away and no one really talks to me or checks in with me a great deal so I felt very lonely.

When I was doing my last frozen IVF treatment I began to really think about the fact that this IVF round may not work and I don't have anyone that lives near me that I can talk to about my childlessness with or connect with.

I approached a friend I knew who went to the local church group to see whether she/they would help me get a group started in the village. She explained it would come under the church group but it wouldn't be a religious group, which for me was good because I'm not religious — also, I don't want to offend anyone. I believe in something but not sure quite what!

I was a little worried about this meeting starting as I may well have been pregnant but that obviously didn't work out, so I was so grateful to get this group started.

Six weeks, a few meetings with my friend, a few marketing ideas later and 'Journeying Together' was born – wow. So, my group is based on supporting one another through childlessness and fertility challenges, a caring and supportive group for anyone experiencing the painful reality of childlessness. Whatever the stage of your journey, you're not alone.

I can't tell you how proud I am of myself but don't get me wrong, this isn't a group I ever wanted to start, and I can assure you the members never wanted to join but, we all have a safe space to talk to one another about a subject that we all sadly share.

Myself and the lady who helped me set the group up talked about how we will conduct the meetings. Introducing and sharing our stories and letting people just talk and be heard is all that is needed and knowing they are not alone. I tell her all about this book I had read called 'Living the Life Unexpected' by Jody Day and that some of the stuff in it is extremely helpful. It's basically a 12-week guide to your Plan B for a meaningful and fulfilling future without children. Now I'm fully aware that people who come to the meeting are still on Plan A, so this book is just a guide as some of the chapters are helpful and have good exercises to help us think differently. I'm still on Plan A if I'm honest, I'm trying to live my life still; until I go through menopause and I know it's final, I'll never give up hope and I know it's the same for a lot of ladies.

The first meeting was to be held on the first Tuesday of January 2020. I was full of excitement and anxiety about meeting new people, but I had to remember they're in the same boat. We hired a room in the community centre, we set up tea, coffee and biscuits and made it a welcoming room because I'm positive anyone coming to a support group for the first time will be just as anxious as me.

The first and second meetings are a success with people turning up, but we're a little rocky in feeling ok to share with each other. As we start to share more and more, we open up more and we all realise no one is judging us in this group and it's a completely safe space.

We try and talk about a particular subject to direct the group meetings so we can all touch on something that we want to talk about or share. Every single one of us has a completely different story as to why we are there and for me, it's nice to feel like I'm not alone and I can talk and speak my mind without being judged.

The group has been running a year now but due to the Coronavirus, we do Zoom meetings which are great as we still feel connected and we also have a WhatsApp and Facebook group so we can all connect on a daily/weekly basis if one of us feel like we need to reach out, that way no one has to wait for the monthly meeting and feel like they're alone for a long time. I now class every one of them as a friend and someone I could call or text if I felt down and that is priceless to me- I've found my tribe. Sadly the lady who helped me run the group can't do this any longer so I now run it myself which is stressful, but fun as I can put my own spin on things with lots of positivity.

After my last ever IVF round had failed, I began to feel like a complete failure again; you start to feel useless and insignificant in this world. I truly believe this feeling is what spurred me on this time to do the volunteering at the nursery and start this group. I felt I needed to have a purpose so I couldn't feel totally useless anymore and it did work, none of it is what I wanted to do, and it took some serious inner strength to push my dream of having children aside to care for my mental state of health and get out there and help other people.

After every failed IVF round or loss, I know I started to feel angry, sad and annoyed, and all these unpleasant feelings that I couldn't shake. So, I googled, what is wrong with me? Why am I having all these horrible emotions? I came across a site that was to do with grief. Now here's the thing; if you've ever read up on grief, they say there are five stages; it's called the Kubler-Ross Model and they are:

- Denial
- Anger
- Bargaining
- Depression
- Acceptance

This might sound crazy to you but think back to a time you 'lost' something. It could have been something as small as a keepsake ring, a watch or something as big as your baby, house or partner. Now think about the emotions you went through during those times and I bet you went through, maybe not in the order, some or all of the stages above at some point.

I have referred to having 'lost' something in the sense of a tangible object, but you can put the grief stages into non-tangible as well. For example, you lost your job, a marriage, your life crutch (i.e. drinking/smoking) or a friendship. Now you can see that anything you lose in life that meant something significant to you is a form of grief and you must grieve your loss to be able to effectively, and in a sense, 'move forward' with the next stage of your life in a healthier way.

There will be times when you think back to your loss or something is said or done that triggers your thoughts about your loss and you have a wobble and perhaps re-live one of the stages. That's okay because if you're aware of what's happening and that you're grieving, you can deal with it better; you know these emotions won't last and it's just a process. Just know you shouldn't bury or not deal with the process because it will come back, you must let your emotions come out, however, they wish, and let them be there until you no longer have the strong emotions. Just sit with them. Don't go back or start drinking or using drugs as this makes a bad situation worse.

So, can you now see how not being able to have children is a 'loss'? It's a lifetime loss and a lifetime of adjustment. You can never just say, "Okay I can't have children so I will move on and do something else now." It just doesn't happen like that. You inevitably go through some or all of these stages of grief about:

- Not being able to conceive naturally.
- Not being able to conceive through IVF or another way.
- All of your friends are starting to have children and you can't relate to them anymore.
- Losing your friends.
- Sadness for your parents who can't be grandparents.
- Your relationship won't be connected with having your own family.
- Your own family enjoying your sibling's children and you're left out.
- You won't go through a pregnancy, a birth, enjoy telling everyone your news, shopping for your new baby, turning a room into a nursery or have a baby shower.

- You can't have that bond with a child and a bond with your own mum/dad through that child.
- You won't experience the life-changing effects of a new baby or take any pictures/videos or enjoy experiences with your new family.
- You won't see them on their first day of nursery, school, middle school, college, university, first tooth, first holiday, first smile, first Christmas or first birthday- the list is endless.
- You won't see them get married or have their own children.
- You will never be called 'mum or dad' or be a part of society in this way.
- You will never be a grandmother or grandfather.

So, you can see the above is a lifetime event; it doesn't just stop with the first process of the grief at not being able to conceive. The grief continues throughout every stage of your life.

In your 20s or 30s your friends may be having babies and doing things with their new family. You sadly won't be a part of that because you will either be battling with the fact you have a period every bloody month and sobbing your heart out or doing crappy rounds of IVF/treatment which, for me, was yet more disappointment. All you really want to say to friends or family who thought you were being selfish is, "I'm sorry if I missed your child's first birthday or I wasn't there for you during your pregnancy or I couldn't bring myself to go to your child's birthday, but I was struggling with my life change of not having what you've got and I'm struggling on my own because this is not normal in society. What you're doing is normal with your children and family, I'm left to the wayside to navigate this utter torment of a life I've been left with."

Then there's your 40s and 50s, watching your friends enjoy their children grow into adults and make their own life going to college or university and eventually they enjoy their children as adults in their life. This is the stage, being childless, that I'm sure I will enjoy seeing my friends again. Their children will be flying the nest and they will be adjusting to a life without their kids (like I have been my entire life) and so will begin to enjoy a bit of time for themselves, going out, etc. I have no doubt they will grapple with 'empty nest syndrome'. Well hello, people my nest has been well and truly empty my entire life so put into context how you feel now is how I've felt forever — lost and alone except you do have kids!

Then there is your 60s and 70s, and enjoying your children's children as a grandparent. Yep, that's a stage that I know I will lose my friends all over again because the talk will inevitably be about their new grandchild. You can't deny them that joy, but you can certainly hide and protect your heart from the pain that will come from hearing these wonderful life-changing events you will never be part of. I can imagine when I am at this stage, it will bring up all my sadness and bring back grief and memories which I will have to work through again.

I have also thought about the fact that I may well be alone when I'm in my 80s or 90s and therefore have tailored my will to reflect that idea. I mean who knows what will happen, but I certainly don't have anyone to leave any money or belongings to unless Simon outlives me. If Simon passes before me, I intend to leave any money to the sausage dog charities because that will be the best legacy I can think of leaving and I know they will be grateful to receive it. Is this something you would ever think about if you didn't have children? I didn't until this happened to me. Perhaps this book will also be a legacy. Who knows?

Also don't forget, those of us who don't have our own family find Mother's Day, Father's Day, Halloween, and Christmas especially hard. It's a constant reminder every year throughout the year that we don't have our own children to share these special times with — a lovely kick in the balls or uterus! So, do us a favour; send us a text or email just say, "I understand today is hard for you, I'm here if you want a chat." You'll have no idea how much that means to receive such a kind message and to know someone is thinking of us on these days.

Take a minute to think about men who also go through the same thing. The emphasis is always on women because they're the ones who carry the child, but men also feel loss when their partner loses a baby or struggles to conceive or when they have their own fertility probelm. I'm pleased to say that Fertility Network UK has set up a group for men-only support and they're starting to get the notice they deserve.

Lastly, I would like to question people who have children and ask: "Why didn't you just adopt?" This is the question childless people or people struggling to conceive get. Your answer is the same as ours, "Because we want our own family."

I, and I'm sure other childless people realise, you're just suggesting this option as a way of having a family, but I need to explain something to you. Adoption is not for everyone and it's a long and personally invasive process that is not to be taken lightly. You will, by now, realise (from what I've told you) that IVF and other routes of trying to conceive are long, invasive, expensive and exhausting processes and you never want to give up hope that your dream will happen.

Don't get me wrong I think that adoption or fostering is an amazing route to go down, but you have to be mentally and physically ready to deal with this process. You have to have stopped IVF for at least six months and not be trying to conceive or wanting to do IVF or other procedures in the future. Basically, you have to be happy with your life as it is before you can take on the process of accepting an adopted child into your world. You have to be realistic that the adoptive child could come with several challenges which you hadn't thought about. It's not as simple as going along to a store and picking a child off the shelf I'm afraid. It's another new process and one that requires some serious thought on everyone's part.

So next time you want to just suggest adoption to your childless family member or friend, think about what you're saying and stop telling childless people they can 'just adopt' like it's a new idea — trust me we've heard of it. You're asking us to give up our dream of having our own family... ummm, yes, the appropriate word here is: RUDE!

Chapter 12
The Sausage Dog Mum

If you've ever owned a sausage dog, you'll know what I'm talking about when I say their little personalities just melt your heart. Even the most hardened man will fall in love with these little bundles of sausage-y cuteness. They're naughty as fuck as well as they don't do anything you tell them to and bark at the bloody wind, but I love them. If yours isn't like that then you are bloody lucky.

During our times of utter despair and having to cope with watching our babies suffer and recover from major back surgeries, I discovered a wonderful lady on Facebook called

Charlotte Baldwin. She was just starting up an amazing charity to help sausage dogs to recover in comfort who have had back surgeries. She sends out buggies, crates, support leads and booties. The Charity is called Dedicated to Dachshunds with IVDD-

www.dedicatedtodachshunds.co.uk
www.facebook.com/Dedicatedtodachshunds.

This was a complete godsend as trying to carry the little buggers was near on impossible after surgery. Being able to give them the chance to go out for fresh air after major surgery and not further injure themselves was amazing.

Here's the caption from Charlotte and you can see the amazing buggy with the dogs in.

I can't express to you how hard it is to watch your baby go through operations and recovery. I can only guess it's the same for your child. My emotions and deep love just make me want to do everything for them and give them the best life possible. I would go to the end of the earth and back for them; they're not just dogs, they have their own personality and special love for you. They rely on you for their every need and they are there for you during every happy and hard time of your life whilst they are alive. A dog cannot be replaced by another dog. Each dog gives you their own love and joy and they're completely unique.

You have to understand that we don't have any children to give all this love to that we have within us so all we can do is give that love to our sausage dogs and that's what we do! You may think we are mad but quite frankly, we don't care.

People have said disgusting things after their operations or Poppy's death, like, "Can't you just get another one," or "What a waste of money." It's just darn right cruel when someone needs support at such a hard time to say such harsh hurtful things. You'd never say that to someone whose kid was going through surgery or just died. The old saying goes, "If you've not got anything nice to say, don't say anything at all." Damn right!

I can't explain how hard it is to go through recovery with your baby dog. I guess just think of the one person you absolutely love to bits and imagine them having all this happening to them. You wake up every day worrying about them and if they will recover, you do anything for them like physio and hydrotherapy even though it costs a bomb! You have appointment after appointment with the vets, surgeons, nurses, physiotherapists and all you want to do is take them on holiday down the beach and watch them enjoy themselves. Not bloody appointments! It starts to feel like doing IVF again, there is no let-up in our lives. Grrr.

So now we have lost our beloved Poppy Pop Pops, Millie Moo is having to get used to living without her as well. It's hard on all of us, and still is as you don't ever forget your baby; she is in my heart and thoughts every day.

Millie Moo is struggling and seems extremely lethargic and just not herself. After seeing the vet for Moo's yearly vaccinations, she just confirmed that Moo was going through a grieving process herself. She was with Poppy for nine years and it will take her time to adjust to this new life without her by her side. Aww, Moo I know I don't have four legs but I give good kisses and cuddles.

It broke my heart but I tried to keep her spirits up as much as I could by taking her on different country walks, trips to the coffee shop, going over to see family, playing with her and just cuddling her – "Coffee Millie Moo?"

Christmas 2019 was just the worst Christmas; it was the first without Poppy and we were utterly miserable from the year just gone but we got through it as best we could.

I started to think about how I could make a good life with just me and Moo. We were both sitting on the sofa not doing a lot of anything, everything had come to an end it seemed I'd finally made it — I was a bum! Ha-ha. Ok no, no I can't do that forever. Think, think, think... ummm.

So over Christmas 2019, I thought about how I could make a business that included looking after Millie Moo. I haven't said earlier in the book but back after I did my first IVF, I didn't allow myself any time to grieve the process and immediately wanted to change things. I knew we were in no position for me to give up work so I decided to start a weekend sausage dog boarding business, this is when I had both Poppy and Millie Moo.

I got my licence from the council and set up a website and I was ready, I was desperate for it to work so it would fill my weekends with not thinking about the fact I couldn't get pregnant cause let's face it... dogs are way better (yes I have totally offended half the population now). I had enquiries but the problem was people wanted to book their dog in for a week at a time rather than a weekend and it never took off. Simon was also conscious of having other people's dogs around both of ours because they had had back surgery and he didn't want other dogs jumping on them and causing another slipped disc so he wasn't overly happy with the idea.

Fast forward to December 2019 and thinking along these lines, I already had half set things up from the last time; I had the perfect opportunity as I wasn't working now. It had been a good seven months since the miscarriage so I had given myself time to work through things to such a degree that I could now think about some sort of future and what I should do. I mean being a bum is great but there is honestly only so much TV you can watch!

I spoke to Simon about it and he agreed it would now be a perfect opportunity to carry out that dream because we only have Millie Moo, I don't work so can do this full-time and I can set it up properly. I was over the moon. And so, the Long Dog Hotel business was born.

Sadly, I had to say goodbye to volunteering at the local nursery because I couldn't dedicate one day during the week if I had sausages coming over to stay. The manager at the nursey understood but was really sad to see me go, they actually wanted to offer me a job there. How lovely is that? I felt proud of myself for overcoming my fear of being around children and to be offered a job really boosted my confidence.

So here's the thing, we know Millie Moo has IVDD and we know how horrible and distressing it is for the doggy parents so I have based my business with that in mind because I would have loved to find a sausage dog only boarding hotel who knows about IVDD to put my babies in whilst I went on holiday. I did my research and realised there isn't anyone who offers this service and there are a lot of dachshunds with IVDD.

I decided to offer respite for dogs who have IVDD, for the dog parents who want to go on holiday and leave their daxi baby with someone who knows and understands the signs of IVDD and this means I will take on fewer dogs at a time to keep their baby safe. I also do dog boarding for sausages and very small breed dogs who don't suffer from IVDD as well because there are plenty of weeks in the year and I'm open all year round.

I spoke to the council got all the information I needed to set up the safest boarding business. There was a mountain of paperwork to go through to make sure I had everything set up properly. First things first I enrolled onto a course to get my OFQUAL Regulated Level 3 Professional Day Care and Boarding accreditation because if you have this qualification it immediately gives you good knowledge and a higher star rating with the council. I passed this — not sure how as I was never that great at doing coursework!

So now the fun part. I set to work creating my website and my business cards to carry about with me. www.longdoghotel.co.uk

Time to get marketing. I set up an Instagram account — no fucking clue but manage to do this. Then it's Twitter's turn. I know it doesn't seem that hard to all the young people out there but holy cow, what a nightmare to work this shit out. (longdoghotel10), (@longdoghotel).

I then had my inspection... dun, dun, dun. Phew, the lady was actually lovely and really helpful. I passed with flying colours and got a 4-star 2-year licence — woo hoo. The only reason I didn't get 5 stars is because they don't have any past data on me for how I run the business so I should get 5 stars on my next review — amazeballs.

After a few weeks of working out all these new platforms, I've finally got the hang of it and we are starting to get a lot of followers and emails from potential new clients. I start to get a lot of hits on my website and boom, people are wanting to book us in time for their summer holiday.

I'm so excited but nervous this dream is finally coming true, what an amazing business I'm going to create. Millie Moo is the Director and other sausages are only allowed to stay when they've had their meet and greet with Moo. If she likes them, they're allowed to stay.

Our first ever client is Banjo, he is adorable and his owners are lovely. Please do check him out on Twitter- @Banjothesausage he gets up to all sorts of naughtiness. He is the perfect client and we all have fun when he comes to stay.

In the meantime, we have lots of meet and greets and a few bookings are coming in but sadly the world has been hit with coronavirus which meant we had to immediately shut down and cancel all bookings. I was totally gutted but it did come to an end and we've had some of our buddies back to play.

I decided that as I can't pursue the business at the moment, I would offer my services (for free) to two charities that I absolutely love. They are called:

The Red Foundation :
www.theredfoundation.net

Dachshund Rescue:
www.dachshundrescue.org.uk

They are both emergency dachshund rescue charities and take on sausages who have IVDD, plus sausages from people who can no longer cope or who have passed away. They pay for the rehabilitation of the sausage and try to find them good homes for adoption. If they can't find an immediate home I have, along with an army of helpers up and down the UK, offered to be a foster mum. We are yet to foster any sausages but we are ready for if we get asked to… the risk is I end up with a load of sausages and I want to keep them all. Ohh sausagey heaven. Never mind I have a huge soft spot for disabled and elderly sausages in need anyway… come to me my pretties.

Yes, it's official: I'm the mad sausage dog lady ha-ha. I have a lot of sausage dog-related items in my house but it's all part of being a great sausage dog mummy. I absolutely love my Millie Moo to bits, she has helped me see there is a point to my existence on this godforsaken Earth, even if it's a small existence, I'm here and I'm doing okay.

Not everyone loves dogs but she's more than just a dog, she is part of my story and I now won't go anywhere without her by my side. If you don't like Millie Moo then you don't like me because we come as a package, she's my sidekick... simples.

There's something about caring for all living things whether human or not that relates to empathy, love, kindness and compassion; all traits that people are naturally drawn to. So, I have to say I personally don't trust people who don't like dogs or have compassion for animal welfare. There must be something missing within that person, how can you not care about animals who don't have a voice? Strange people.

My Long Dog Hotel has to be the best outcome made from such a terrible set of circumstances and, I don't know if anyone else is, but I'm proud of myself. You go girl (pat on the back).

I have come a long way from such constant and utter despair and sadness in my life that I'm starting to feel like a butterfly rather than an ugly chrysalis for sure.

Can I get some love from you all? 'Cause, that's what I need to keep going on this journey.

Why thank you, people.

Chapter 13
Endo surgery... what, again?

I was very aware that since the beginning of 2020 I had lots of pain in my uterus again so I trundled off back to my GP who said that I will need to go for an MRI to confirm that it is endo that is causing the problem — really? I know that my symptoms are endo and I know how bad they are but whatever. Grrr.

Role on March 2020 and I've had several scans but now an MRI — man I hate those machines; if you're claustrophobic then forget it! They sound like you're in a loud nightclub with a bad DJ! After that delightful experience, I had to wait a further six or eight weeks before the surgeon called me to confirm that I do have my delightful endo back at stage 4 (brilliant) and he thinks it's on my bladder and bowel (even more brilliant). Any non-urgent surgery is on hold because of the pandemic at the moment and I'm on the waiting list which he said was about a 6-month wait but he would call in a few months with an update. Oh, the joy of joys — more waiting around.

The surgeon called me in August to confirm that due to the pandemic they're not opening any operations up this year! Hold on, so does this mean it's a longer wait? I'm then told it's over a year wait due to all the backlog. I get off the phone and have a bit of a meltdown; I'm 37 already and with every year that passes I know I have less and less chance of trying to conceive naturally… why, oh why is this happening?

So now I'm stuck between a rock and a hard place, I can't have the surgery on the NHS unless I wait almost two years which entails sitting around enduring worse pain and by which time, I'll be 39 and seriously unlikely to conceive — sounds fab! Or we look into paying for the operation privately.

The lovely husband knows waiting around is not viable for me and us, so we discuss going down the private route. I do lots of research online and come across a lady in an endometriosis Facebook group who had surgery with a chap in London based at The Endometriosis Clinic in central London and she's raving about him. She sends me all the details and we have an extensive conversation about her journey. I look at all options and ultimately, I know if I'm paying for this, I want to get the best guy possible doing the job because I don't want to pay twice.

It turns out there are several women who've had surgery with this chap, so I'm now talking on a message group to all these women for a few weeks. I do think to myself I would rather know some of his patients and get first-hand accounts than just use someone blindly because of reviews on their website. He's one of the best surgeons in the endo world and does robotic excision surgery which is extremely specialised.

The trouble is the only way to find out how much it costs is to have a consultation and a scan which is £785 ($1060) off the bat before I've even made a decision! Jesus, I knew this would be expensive. The cost of surgery is dependent on how extensive your endo is. If it's on your bowel and bladder, for example, that will obviously be a more complicated surgery and therefore cost more. Typical.

After a trip to London to have a scan which was rather expensive and uncomfortable who do you think needs complicated surgery? Yes, you guessed it: me! "Oh yes, Mrs Light, you have endo on your bowel, bladder and ovaries." Fan-dabie-dozie. Yes, it has come back with a vengeance.

This pain became quite bad and has come back within two years of the last surgery, which again is very quick for endo; they say you should get about five years before you might need another surgery and this was all since I stopped doing IVF. I don't know if this is a factor but in my head, the hormone IVF drugs probably didn't help in feeding the endo to come back fully after I stopped pumping myself with the IVF drugs. Who knows? However, we've made a conscious decision not to do anymore IVF ever again. Weirdly, drawing a line under it feels good, knowing I won't have to endure going through any of that heartache and pain again is a relief.

A week after my scan, I have my zoom consultation with the doctor; he goes through all the options in great detail and talks through my scan with me. The options are:

1. Hysterectomy.
2. Excision surgery just on the bladder and any other endo in the uterus and shaving off the bowel endo as much as he can.
3. Excision surgery on the bladder, the other endo in the uterus and bowel resection.

Hmmm, decisions to make! So, option 1 is not an option because I really do want an opportunity to have children, even if it's small. Option 2 is the best for preserving fertility and making the bowel endo more comfortable. Option 3 also good for preserving fertility but could have massive complications that are unforeseen with having a bowel resection — plus that is like having two big operations at once.

We go with option 2 so I will be the most comfortable and if the bowel endo gives me any jip in the next few years then I'll have to make that decision if I want my bum cut up or not!

£12,000 ($15,927) paid out later and we have a date of October 3rd 2020 – feeling very poor but so very glad I'm having this done. It's amazing how quickly you get things when you pay for them.

Obviously, the pandemic has made things strange so I can't go into hospital with anyone, just on my own which gave me massive anxiety. I mean what if I have complications there is no one to hug me waaaaa… it's okay, I'll take my teddy problem solved. My husband drops me off at 6:30 am at a very posh private hospital in central London where I'm escorted to my private room to get comfortable. The next picture is of the room, with private bathroom, TV and a view of the street. I unpack my things, get comfortable on the bed put the TV on, set up my iPad then a lovely nurse comes in to go through things with me. She tells me to put on the gown and socks provided and gives me a menu so I can choose what food I would like for when I come around.

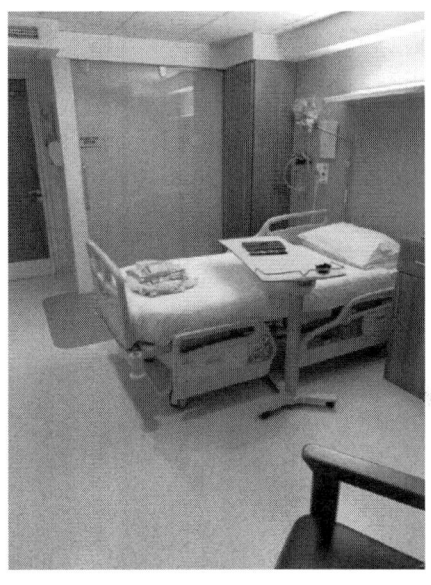

I have to say, the menu is bloody amazing! It's like posh restaurant options. Obviously, chocolate ice-cream is a must. When she comes back, I give her my choices and I'm all set ready to go down to surgery at 9 am. The doctor comes in at 8:30 am to check my options and have me sign paperwork and explain what will happen.

I sit waiting for someone to collect me at 9 am I've got butterflies in my stomach I'm so nervous about it all. The nurse comes in and I walk with her to the elevator, go down to the operation theatre and the anaesthetist begins his routine. I sit on the edge of the bed, let my left hand drop down and he tells me to look away whilst he inserts the needle. In the meantime, there is another anaesthetist behind me who lifts my gown puts some cold gel onto my back and lets me know that he will be inserting the needle into my back and I shouldn't feel a thing. It is at this point, I have no recollection of what happened but I do know a load of futuristic robots took over removing the horrible endo disease- good ridden.

I wake up in the recovery lounge with an insatiable thirst, my head is spinning, and I'm shaking uncontrollably. A nurse is sitting beside my bed who tends to my every need, keeping me warm, giving me more morphine and some water. I'm told to relax then I will be wheeled back up to my room shortly; they're just monitoring me for the moment.

At about 1ish I'm back in my room and feeling numb. A nurse comes in to check me and let me know that the doctor will be around to check I'm okay. Sure enough, he is. He says it all went really well, he had to put a catheter bag in to give my bladder a rest for a few weeks, but he will be back tomorrow to go over the surgery with me.

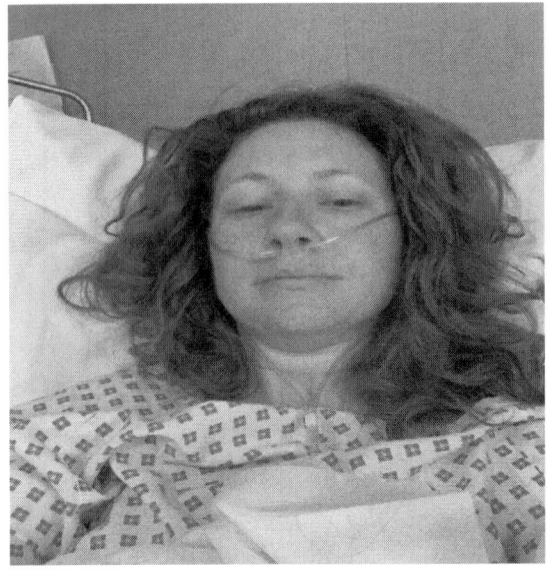

The rest of the day I'm just exhausted, but I speak with my husband and family to put their minds at rest. I have morphine on tap and if I'm feeling sore, I just click the button and I'm immediately pumped. The nurse keeps coming in to check on me every few hours and take my vitals, sadly I have very low blood pressure so I didn't get any sleep and I can assure you, having a catheter in didn't help with getting comfortable.

The next day, the doctor came around to see me and gave me a rundown of what he did and show me a delightful video of the robot cutting away at my uterus; it's pretty gross and I could see my husband going a funny shade over Zoom. the doctor said if I was feeling okay and my blood pressure was stable, I could go home after dinner that day. Well, that was amazing news, but I wanted to wait until the afternoon to make that decision.

I rested up and managed to eat some more ice-cream, sandwiches, etc, drink lots of tea before the nurse and I decided that I could go home to my husband and sausage dogs. We agreed on 8 pm. The nurse had to come and give me a bag of painkillers for the next few weeks, instructions a catheter stand and new bags.

I couldn't stand up straight as I had four incision holes that were covered over on my stomach. The picture below is just two of the holes — ouchy!

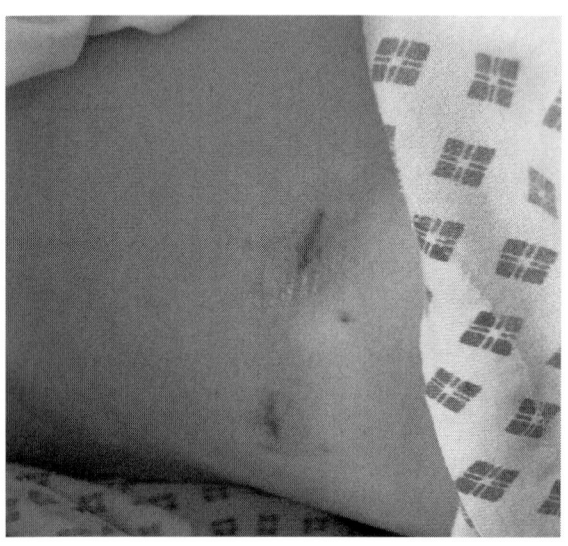

So like the hunchback of Notre Dame, I collect my belongings and drugs and walk out of the hospital to meet my husband. I was so very glad to be going home to my own bed.

Getting in bed was interesting because the catheter bag had to be put on a stand below my bed so it could drain down. The tube was strapped to the side of my left leg which meant I could only lie on my back. I was in a lot of pain on my stomach so I couldn't lie any other way but I did get a night's sleep unlike in the hospital. My poor husband was very worried about the catheter emptying properly and it was all extremely overwhelming for him having to deal with the house, his job, the sausage dogs, take me up to London and now I have this new piss bag situation to deal with which made him faint for two seconds on the floor of our bedroom the first night. Luckily, he'd decided to lie down beforehand!

The next few days were the absolute worst; I felt horribly sick because of the blood pressure and couldn't keep anything down, I was very sore and feeling sorry for myself. It got a lot better and by end of week two, I had nailed this piss bag thing so I didn't get any infections and I didn't even use the really strong drugs provided. We went back up to London after two weeks and I had the catheter removed and that was so, so good to have that bloody thing out! They checked my bladder by scan and said it has all healed so I can just take it easy for the next few weeks.

At week four I was feeling absolutely amazing. I've never woken up not in any of my usual pain but it's all gone and I'd never been happier. I'm aware that the body could take a while to sort itself out and I had a few niggles with a bit of pain and a longer period cycle but I'm in no pain, yippie.

I'm only a few months post-surgery (Dec 2020) and I feel like a normal woman. I cannot tell you how amazing it is to have my health back and to not feel so down and upset because of the chronic pain I was in. The doctor had said to me, as soon as I'm well enough, get trying to make a baby naturally… okay, will do!

This operation was more about feeling better for me; fertility was secondary, and it would be a miracle if it did happen. The fertility journey began in 2012 so turn the last two numbers around you've got 2021 which hopefully will signify the end of my fertility journey — in a good way. Keep praying and wishing for me, 2021 could be the year!

Chapter 14

Who am I now?

Well exactly, who am I now? Well, I know one thing, all these 'events' in my life have changed me as a person. I'm not as tolerant of people as I once was; I have a new-found respect for looking after number one and not worrying so much about what others think about me. I think traumatic life events profoundly change you in ways you never thought about before. I'm old enough and ugly enough to make my own decisions irrespective of anyone else and that's the way I think now. If you don't make number one happy first, then no one will stand a chance of making you happy.

This definitely isn't the life I wanted to have, I had bigger 'happier' plans for myself, but they were taken away from me and are completely out of my control. It saddens me that others can just be so brash and say "be happy with what you've got." Yes, thank you for that really shit suggestion you clearly have no idea about but think you can suggest that I should just be happy. People just don't understand that it takes time for someone to accept their options and move to a happier state of being, it doesn't happen over night, it's a process that only you can do and no amount of someone telling you to do it will help. You need to do that in your own time when you're ready, not when someone else tells you.

These sorts of comments usually come from people who already have children and a happy existence knowing they've got them and I'd say, "Well how would you feel if you didn't have your children?" Probably pretty miserable if that's what you wanted to have but couldn't have them, so welcome to my world. What an utterly small-minded, unsympathetic, uncaring, nasty, shitty thing to say to someone who has or is struggling, usually for years to have a family. It's a very close minded look at the world and their behaviour, don't you think?

Little do they know I'm dying inside and the times they don't see me, I'm buying stocks and shares in Kleenex, but no one wants to see sad posts all of the time all over their social media pages or by text or even in person. I don't want to be that person who brings people down and burdens them with my life problems. I hide behind my 'happy' fake exterior and get on as best I can with my life, secretly hoping I get my dream one day before it's too late. But I live with the tedious ups and downs every month thinking this is the month it will happen and then it doesn't. I also hope the dream happens before the dreaded menopause sets in, which in my case, is going to be early because I have low ovarian reserve anyway — bloody brilliant, something to look forward to.

Then you get the parents who, when you do indulge in a small conversation about their children just for politeness (for one fleeting second) decide this type of conversation is what you want to hear and proceed to say things like, "Oh, trust me you don't want children, they are just so expensive," or "It's a bloody nightmare organising them to do anything." Jesus people, think about who you're sharing this very information with. The childless would absolutely love, I mean we long to be doing any of that insignificant shitty stuff with our own kids so stop bloody moaning about what you've got, and start enjoying it because no doubt you have beautiful children to indulge in. I get your children are hard work, but you choose to have them in your life, you had a choice, I didn't get that choice, so you definitely don't have a right to moan about them.

I have learnt that you definitely can't change people and how you think they should be towards you; all you can do is choose to accept the way they are or put that relationship to bed and say goodbye. We are on this Earth for such a short amount of time, there isn't time to waste on people who are not as nice to you as you are to them. Sadly during difficult events in your life, you will learn who your true friends and family are. They're the ones who, even if it's only occasionally, check-in and make sure you're doing okay, or offer to help you out during a crisis or to take you out for the day to cheer you up or send you something nice. Defo keep them ones close cause who doesn't love a present or cake? I don't mind either, by the way.

I have made some new and wonderful friends during my journey and have lost old friends. The new friends have made up for the losses and I guess it's a bit like going through school, college, university and jobs in your life. You make new friends; you drift apart from old friends and sometimes you say goodbye because you didn't need that negativity in your life, and you know what- that's okay because that is self-care and growth for you.

I'm currently building a new suitcase that's full of joyful things to do and I'm beginning to feel a bit happier these days. I'm not completely out of the pit of despair though and I don't believe I ever will be. I will always have one foot in that grave because when people touch the sensitive scar on my heart, it sadly sends me down into the pit for a bit. I hope as time goes on, I don't spend as long in the pit when my scar is hurting, and I can pull myself out and open my suitcase full of goodies. I know this is a lifetime change but as long as I protect my heart and my emotions and learn to deal with them the best way I know how then my mental health is all that matters.

I've learnt, and I'm sure you can already tell, that I have a serious passion for sausage dogs and especially the elderly and disabled ones. I have created my business from that passion, and I hope (after the coronavirus) that it continues to grow. Millie Moo will continue to suffer from IVDD for the rest of her life and I aim to make her as comfortable and as spoilt as possible.

She turned 10 years old in January 2021 bless her so she will be spoilt and loved as much as possible because who knows how much time I will get with her, every moment is precious.

I will continue to not amuse my 'shit friend' because this keeps me happy and healthy and I really don't like hangovers anymore. I hope some of you join me down that beautiful road and I would absolutely love to hear from you if you do.

I'm starting to be okay with this body of mine; it's the only one I've got, and I need to look after it from now on. I know it has let me down so far for baby-making but I figure I shouldn't punish it by filling it full of hateful crap like alcohol and caffeine or cigarettes and make it feel bad. I need to be kind to it, so I'll fill it with chocolate cake instead which definitely does make you feel happier, that's for sure.

I'm only 37 so I figure I may, if I'm lucky, have 5-10 years of ovary life yet so I won't give up hope that we will have a family one day, even with endometriosis (which hopefully won't come back too soon).

Who knows what the future holds for any of us. All I know is right now, in time, it wouldn't be fair to go down the adoption route for us or the child because I still hold a torch for my own family and I'm not sure that light will go out until I finally go through the menopause and my body tells me this is the end.

It has taken me all these years to get to a point where I'm okay to start doing things to make myself a bit happy again. 2021 for me is the year to get back on track. Start my business going again, get back in touch with friends, keep my fertility group going, publish this book, do some fertility interviews and get my story in the local paper. Starting all of these things has helped me as part of my healing process for myself so far this year, even during lockdown.

Sadly, everything in everyone's world has been put on hold due to coronavirus but I've adapted to a temporary routine. I have volunteered to cut scrub patterns, make masks, and premature baby hats for our village sewing group to send to our local hospital and care homes; we're also making little angels and teddy masks for the children's ward — as modeled by Millie Moo below. We're now looking at making it into a charity with myself (coughs) on the member's board — winner!

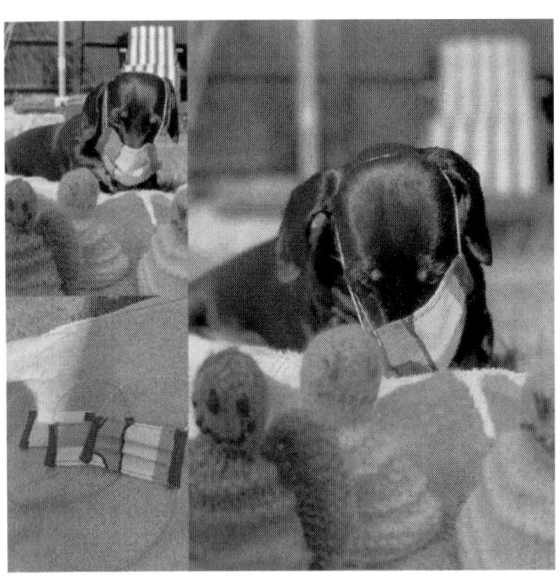

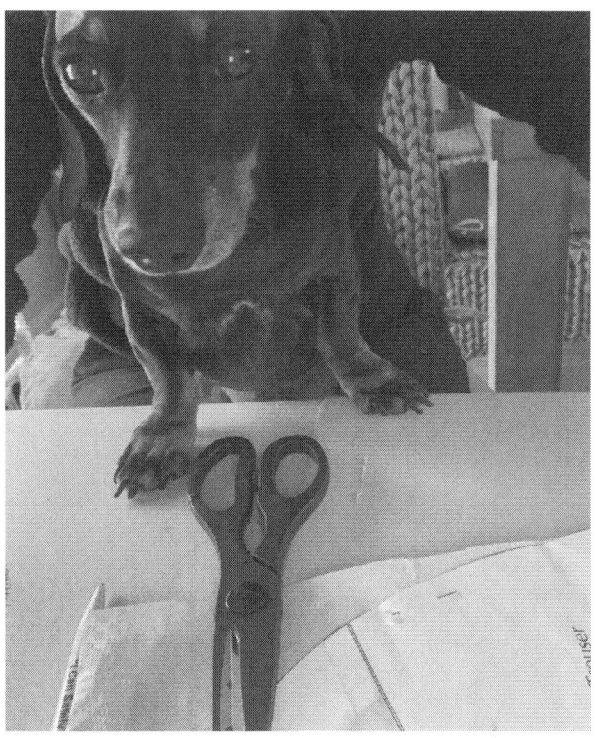

Me and Moo cutting scrub patterns!

At the beginning of June, we decided to rescue a new friend for Millie Moo so she wouldn't be so depressed. She is called Dolly and she is a six-year-old chocolate and tan long-haired sausage dog. She has settled in amazingly well. Here she is... one, two, three... aww.

Millie Moo goes out for her daily walks in her buggy still with Dolly by her side and they have become extremely good friends.

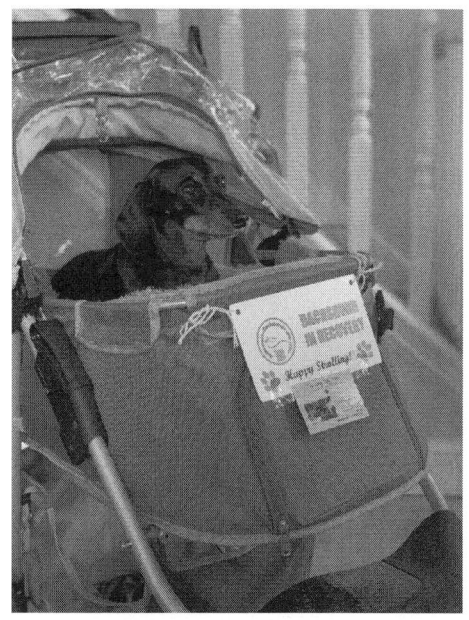

I'm not going to let this virus stop me from progressing and I hope it doesn't stop anyone else either. We may not be in the same boat, but we're all in this river together.

My bit in the local paper... #proud – thumbs up.

There's no end to this book for me. I started down a horrible, congested road full of anger and potholes and I'm now starting to see a bit of that beautiful flower-lined country road.

Just remember, if you're struggling today, you have survived everything you've gone through up to this point. The best days of your life are still yet to come. There are still people you haven't met, and things you haven't experienced.

YOU CAN DO THIS and YOU'VE GOT THIS.

Please do vist the book's facebook page to leave a comment or get in touch.

I'd love to hear from some fans!

Don't forget- #bekind

https://www.facebook.com/lucylightroad

Tick List to Remember

- [ ] Praise someone who has given up the 'shit friend' (alcohol).

- [ ] You don't need to fear anything by not drinking, you have everything to gain so I challenge you to try the 30-day not-drinking challenge and see if you like the pretty countryside road.

- [ ] A dog is not 'just a dog' to the owner, they are family members.

- [ ] The loss of a pet is real and the grief is as intense as losing a human friend/family member.

- [ ] Think before you suggest adoption to anyone.

- [ ] Send kind texts/emails on special days of the year to your childless friend/family reminding them you are thinking of them.

- [ ] Every IVF treatment/other treatment is a loss that is being grieved.

- [ ] The childless have to live this life forever, not just at the 'couldn't conceive' stage.

- [ ] Your childless friend/family member is struggling with fertility and although wants to be invited to things, needs you to say, "It's okay I understand if you don't want to come."

- [ ] Your childless friend/family member would appreciate being told about pregnancy announcements separately and with a kind message of, "I understand this news is hard for you, I am here if you want to talk."

- [ ] Definitely don't tell your childless friend/family member to 'just relax.'

- [ ] Don't suggest to your childless friend/family member that they should 'just be happy with what they've got.'

- [ ] Don't suggest to your childless friend/family member that they can be the best Auntie/Uncle. They don't want to hear that.

- [ ] The next time you're at a party or an event, think about when you ask someone if they have children. This could be a trigger question for some. Approach with caution, tell them about you first before asking questions and get a feel for that person.

- [ ] #Bekind – always, because you don't know what is going on behind that fake happy world any person may be portraying.

Acknowledgements

I would like to say a huge thank you to myself for getting off my lazy bum and actually writing this memoir — it might put a smile on someone's face! I couldn't have done it without my inner strength to push myself forward with my can-do attitude. My editor, Lauren Raybould, from The Night Owl Editing who believed in my book and my friend Katy Stickland.

My husband, Millie Moo the late Poppy and Dolly have also been a massive inspiration in this process. Without them, I wouldn't have had the life I've had so far.

I would also like to thank my friend Manny currently sitting on death row in Florida USA. I started writing to him and he has ignited a writing flame that has kept burning.

I pay tribute to my beautiful nan, Betty, who I know would have been proud of me for what I've achieved so far in my life. She never let life get her down, right until the end and I'd like to think I am just the same.

To Leila and John who have also been a massive part of my life, especially my drinking life and I'm looking forward to being able to have parties (without booze for me) and enjoy everyone's company. And Nick and James my housemates from back in the day for making that part of my life fun and a part of my life I won't forget.

I especially want to thank Del and his mum Pat for being there for us during our absolute desperate moment of need and taking us to their beautiful villa in Spain.

I'd like to thank everyone in the Journeying Together group who have been amazing friends and continue to be.

I thank all the family and friends who were there for us during our times of trauma. Please keep being there, our journey never ended.

Lastly, I'd like to thank the amazing Charlotte Baldwin and Elaine from the charity Dedicated to Dachshunds with IVDD who have also been a major support in our life, helping with Poppy and Millie Moo's recovery.

To donate money to the Infertile, Sober Sausage Mum's appeals please see below:

Sausage Dogs

Dedicated to Dachshunds with IVDD

The Red Foundation

Dachshund Rescue UK

Get A Long Dachshund Rescue (Florida)

Endometriosis

Endometriosis UK

Lucy Light (joke)

Fertility

Fertility Network UK

Where to Find Help

(FB=Facebook)

Alcohol Recovery

Club Sober (FB)

drinkaware.co.uk, aa.org, smartrecovery.org.uk

soberistas.com, livingsober.org.nz, sober-sassy-life.thinkific.com, joinclubsoda.com

mummywasasecretdrinker.blogspot.com, thesoberschool.com

Fertility

Journeying Together (my group- contact me)

Fertility Network UK (FB),

worldchildlessweek.net

Gateway-women.com, thefertilitypodcast.com

Thisisalicerose (Instagram)

Childless Path to Acceptance (FB), Childless Perks (FB), Childless Chit Chat (FB)

Endometriosis

Endometriosis Guidance and Support UK (FB)

Endo Diet Support Group & Natural Remedies (FB)

Miscarriage

miscarriageassociation.org.uk

childbereavementuk.org

Miscarriage After IVF/Fertility Treatment UK (FB)

Loss of a Pet

Bluecross.org.uk, rainbowbridge.com, pet-loss.net

The Rainbow Bridge Pet Loss & Grief Support (FB)

Pet Loss Grief Support (FB)

Printed in Great Britain
by Amazon